CARMANAH

Artistic Visions
of an
Ancient Rainforest

WESTERN CANADA WILDERNESS COMMITTEE

PUBLISHER

SUMMERWILD PRODUCTIONS

and

RAINCOAST BOOKS

PRODUCERS

In the spirit of Emily Carr,
an artist
who understood the value of ancient rainforests,
Western Canada Wilderness Committee
dedicates this book
to the artists and volunteers
who have made the preservation of the
Carmanah Valley
a very real possibility.

Any major book project entails a massive effort on the part of a host of professionals. In this instance, it also involved a small army of volunteers. *Carmanah, Artistic Visions of an Ancient Rainforest* represents a special achievement by everyone concerned because of the time constraint. It took less than four months from when the first material was gathered until copies were on sale in the bookstores.

The positive energy and commitment that everyone gave to this project was most heartening, and in the sincere hope that no one has been forgotten, the Western Canada Wilderness Committee extends its heartfelt thanks to the following contributors. With their help, the Wilderness Committee has launched its most ambitious publishing venture to date.

Without the exceptional efforts of the artists who visited Carmanah, there would be no book. Their response was so overwhelming that there was more artwork offered than could be included in this book. Not only did they donate their works to the project, they produced posters, painted T-shirts, helped arrange the art show tour, and even provided transportation, food, and accommodation for the volunteers. The warmest appreciation possible is extended to all the participating artists.

A similar appreciation is extended to the writers—David Suzuki, Cameron Young, Randy Stoltmann, Adriane Carr, Paul George, Sherry Kirkvold, Arne Hansen, Bruce Cockburn and Ken Budd. Their words tell the fascinating and important story of Carmanah.

The Wilderness Committee is indebted to its advisory committee, which fostered the development of this publication. Joe Foy was ever available to share a balanced perspective. Paul George offered prudent insights into the process. Arne Hansen worked tirelessly, not only as project coordinator for the book, but organizing the touring art show and a documentary film.

The expertise of executive producer Ken Budd of SummerWild Productions must be noted. His patience and professionalism nurtured the project to fruition—and finished the book on time.

Sherry Kirkvold had, in some ways, the most difficult task. It was her responsibility to interview the artists and assist in the writing of their biographies and editing of their statements. All of this material had to be assembled with a mark of perfection in too short a time.

There were a great many people who contributed to making the artists' expeditions a success. Mark Hobson was Vancouver Island coordinator for the project, writing the initial letters to the artists and compiling final lists of those traveling to Carmanah. He was also central to the establishment of the base camp in the valley. Leo De Groot, a trail-building expert, upgraded the access trail into the valley with the help of Sandra Irvine, Bill Munn, Victor Prochaska, Scott Rogers, and Michael Tilitsky.

A dynamo named Lorna Walsh organized the camp and kitchen crews that made everyone so comfortable and produced mountains of delicious food. Assisting her were Barb Abernethy, Jenny Balke, Linda Bassingthwaighte, Alison Campbell, Susan Carr, Darlene Choquette, John Ebell, Nadine Ebell, Peggy Frank, Dennis Kangasniemi, Lynda Laushway, Cheryl MacLean, Tim McGrady, Mary Morden, Ian Rogers, Tristan Rogers, Mary Ronnie, Peggy Sowden, Sonja Teuwen, David Thomson, and Jan Whitehead. Common Loaf Bakery of Tofino and Meg Gillie donated baked goods, and Mr. Grocer in Duncan helped with the purchase of groceries.

Packing food and gear up and down the trail were Herbert Haupt, Scott Rogers, Greg Stoltmann, Randy Stoltmann, Warrick Whitehead, and George Yearsley. Shawnigan Lake School and Dorothy Baert of Tofino Sea Kayaking donated the use of their camping equipment.

In addition to helping out with camp chores and odd jobs in the city, Fiona Gold and Isobel McDonald were first-aid attendants for the expedition.

Four professional photographers produced more than three thousand slides from the weekend events. Generously donating their time and labor were Trevor Mills, Kevin Oke, Jay Squelch and Kaj Svensson.

Back in Vancouver, assisting Sherry Kirkvold with the copying and transcription of audio tapes were William Creelman, Mark Edwards, Gail Landau, and Jack Norrie. Gail Duchene constructed the list of artists for Mark Hobson, and typists were Rochelle Davidson, Karin Jander, Mary Niemi, Dorothy Robertson, and Robin Sousanta. Sarah Khan assisted Arne Hansen.

Melford Bell, Annette Garm, and Fiona Gold expertly handled the difficult task of of collecting the art from the artists.

Annette Garm, with help from Leslie Spence, also did a magnificent job of designing the book launch and gala preview of the art show.

The professional team that produced *Carmanah, Artistic Visions of an Ancient Rainforest* must also be recognized. Alex Green of Alex Studio created the clean, classy design. Elaine Jones handled the tough assignment of editor with aplomb. Trevor Mills photographed the art with professional accuracy. And the staffs at Zenith Graphics, Hemlock Printers, and North-West Book Company, who expertly handled the color separations, electronic imaging, printing, and binding, are to be commended for their dedication and professional expertise.

The spirit of Carmanah provided sustenance for all those who so unselfishly gave to this project. May it be there in future, so that it can continue to do so.

Foreword	*EQUILIBRIUM* *David Suzuki*	9
Preamble	*THE ROOTS OF TIME* *Cameron Young*	10
Introduction	*TRACKING GIANTS* *Randy Stoltmann*	12
History	*CREATION OF A PARK* *Adriane Carr & Paul George*	14
Map	*THE CARMANAH VALLEY* *Nola Johnston*	17
Natural History	*THE TREE-MENDOUS FOREST* *Sherry Kirkvold*	18
The Project	*ONE HUNDRED ARTISTS* *Arne Hansen*	22
The Art		25
Epilogue	*IF A TREE FALLS* *Bruce Cockburn*	166

Equilibrium
David Suzuki

After a lifetime of daydreaming childhood fantasies of visiting the Amazon "jungle," I was finally able to journey there in 1988. The Amazon rainforest was a biologist's dream but offered far more than I imagined: what I also saw was horrifying destruction of the most diverse ecosystem on the planet by dams, burns and bulldozers. Brazilians countered my criticism of rainforest depletion by pointing out that they destroy their forests as a solution to terrible poverty, illiteracy, and massive international debt. Canadians have squandered their rich ecosystems every bit as profligately as the Brazilians, but we don't have the excuse of poverty or lack of education.

Around the world, wilderness is falling at a catastrophic rate before the deadliest predator in the history of life on earth. The statistics are shocking: annually, 90 million human beings are added to the global population while 25 billion tonnes of topsoil erode away; every second, nearly half a hectare (an acre) of tropical rainforest disappears, cumulatively eradicating an estimated twenty thousand species per year. Add widespread pollution of air, water, and soil, atmospheric degradation, and climate change, and we have a recipe for unprecedented global disaster.

We are a species that, through its intelligence, has exceeded its biological constraints but in the process lost its sense of place in the biosphere. Convinced of our knowledge and ability to control nature, we exploit the very life-support systems of the planet in the name of short-term comfort and economic profit. Wilderness is disappearing throughout the world so quickly that each remaining untouched area becomes that much more rare and precious.

It's clear that in the contentious debates over native land claims, conservation, jobs, and profit, there is a major factor that is missing. It cannot be defined or quantified, yet it has far greater importance than anything economic. I am speaking of a spiritual relationship with nature that puts humankind in equilibrium with the rest of the natural world. There are powerful vestiges of such a perspective in indigenous societies throughout the world. Among non-native peoples, science is the most dominant view, but there are echoes of a spiritual attitude that differs radically from the fragmented, linear perspective of science. Poets, artists, and composers tap into other dimensions of human sensation that could provide a counterbalance to the destructive course we have set for ourselves. We desperately need to search for those alternatives to our present priorities.

David Suzuki

A well-known educator, author, and scientist, Dr. David Suzuki has been at the forefront of the global environmental movement for many years.

The Roots of Time
Cameron Young

The chilling winter storm blurred the coastline with a driving rain and hurled jagged-edged waves high on the beach. The gray sand turned to saltwater soup and was sucked into the black ocean.

A very weathered Sitka spruce tree grew at the high-water mark where the forest fringe makes its uneasy peace with the relentless Pacific. For the moment, the tree's top layer of roots lay exposed, scoured by storm.

Onto the beach and into the storm walked a solitary young woman, a small knife held in one hand and a basket in the other. When she reached the tree she dropped to her knees. Soon her basket was filled with lengths of Sitka spruce tree roots. She knew the tree would easily grow new roots, and that it would ride out the storms of winter for years to come.

On her way back to her oceanside house, she passed the abandoned home of her husband's family. Years earlier it had collapsed under the weight of a heavy snow, but one totem pole was still standing. On it was carved an obscure figure with a wide open mouth. In times past, her father-in-law had hooked up a water-line to the pole, and water continually poured out of that huge mouth. The young woman giggled at the fountain totem as she trudged on by.

By summertime, long before it was time to walk the shoreline trails in search of plump salmonberries, the woman had split the spruce roots in half and begun weaving them into immaculate baskets. This was work she did in her spare moments, when she wasn't caring for her husband, her three children, and her husband's mother.

That woman's name was Susan Knighton. Sixty years ago, when she was barely twenty years old, she and her family made their home near the mouth of Carmanah Creek. No one has lived there since. For Susan, Carmanah was the only place she ever really called home. Only she didn't call it Carmanah. She called it Qwa-ba-duwa.

Susan's husband was Frank Knighton, a trapper. When he wasn't tending his seven-mile-long trapline, he would transform long cedar logs into elegant dugout canoes and finely crafted totem poles. He also carved delicate designs on silver bracelets. Susan and Frank Knighton were among the last practitioners of a way of life whose roots reach back perhaps eight thousand years.

Susan Knighton now lives in the village of Nitinat, by the lake of the same name, just outside Pacific Rim National Park. The village itself is about an hour's drive from the magnificent forests of the Carmanah Valley.

When it first became evident in 1988 that MacMillan Bloedel was about to log the giant Sitka spruce of Carmanah, Susan Knighton made one final visit to her valley. Memories of the old days swept over her like the cascading waves of the Pacific.

"I sure like the way it is," she told me one day, generously sharing both her memories and her kitchen table. "It would be a shame to put those trees down. But one person like me can't win I guess."

Twenty years earlier I had slumped down at the foot of a twenty-five-hundred-year-old marble column that is part of the Parthenon in Athens, Greece. It was a hot day in April, the sky was clean and blue, and the white marble sparkled.

The pure simple beauty of the fluted column was captivating, and dozens upon dozens of these elegant works of art were scattered about the sacred hill of the Acropolis. Each column was a perfect 1.9 metres (6 feet, 3 inches) in diameter and 10.4 metres (34 feet, 3 inches) tall.

A soft wind blew through the marble columns and stirred up twenty-five hundred years worth of cultural memories. From democracy to architecture, from philosophy to athleticism, these timeless ruins gently reverberated with the wisdom of the ages.

Symbolically at least, the spot where I was resting was the very foundation of all Western culture. That these marble monuments from antiquity still existed was a miracle. That you could visit here and make direct contact with the roots of Western civilization was a gift of inestimable worth. Visitors from around the world walked silently among the gleaming columns. When they spoke at all, it was in reverential whispers.

Two decades later the memories of that day on the Acropolis flooded over me as I sat at the foot of a Sitka spruce tree in the Carmanah Valley. It was a clear day in April and the bright sun sparkled. The tree formed a perfect column as it sought out the blue sky above.

Much taller and thicker than the marble columns of classical Greece, here was an unpolished elegance that rivaled even the most exquisite pillars of the Parthenon. The Carmanah Valley was filled with these spectacular Sitka spruce, growing in idyllic, fern-laden glens beside a dancing stream of ice-cold water. Visitors from around the world walked silently among the towering trees. When they spoke at all, it was in reverential whispers.

These Sitka spruce, many five hundred years old, anchor a self-perpetuating ecosystem that has been seeking evolutionary perfection for some ten thousand years. Many of the trees approach 3 metres (10 feet) in diameter and are close to 90 metres (300 feet) tall. The biggest spruce of all powers skyward for 95 metres (312 feet). Incredibly, growing in a neighboring valley is at least one western redcedar tree—nearly 6 metres (20 feet) in diameter—that is almost as old as the marble columns of the Parthenon.

The magnificent trees of British Columbia's coastal temperate rainforest are descended from preglacial giants that flourished in western North America over a million and half years ago. After nearly one hundred years of coastal logging, most of this irreplaceable legacy has been clear-cut. Any exceptional forests that remain, such as Carmanah, are living on borrowed time.

A soft wind blew through the tree tops of Carmanah, stirring up cultural memories that have been accumulating for possibly eight thousand years. This was a subtle wind. It didn't speak of the glorification of human accomplishments, but of the harmonies of nature. It spoke of the integration of the natural and human worlds. It spoke of being rooted in the earth. It spoke with a voice Susan Knighton knows intimately.

Clearly, when we come to Carmanah to bear witness to this masterwork of nature, we come not just to marvel, but to learn.

To clear-cut the Carmanah rainforest would be to desecrate a priceless global heritage—the equivalent of bulldozing the Parthenon. Should the day come when Carmanah is threatened, Susan Knighton can be assured that one person like her indeed can win the struggle to save the valley. All of us will see to that.

Adrian Dorst

Of the entire length of Carmanah Creek, only its mouth is protected within the boundaries of Pacific Rim National Park.

Freelance writer Cameron Young, author of the award-winning The Forests of British Columbia, *specializes in writing about the environment.*

Tracking Giants
Randy Stoltmann

A year after the provincial government granted MacMillan Bloedel a tree farm licence giving it tenure over an area of Vancouver Island which included Carmanah, the company sent in a crew to assess this valley's timber. Michael Gye, one of the cruisers on that 1956 survey, later reported seeing a monster Sitka spruce, measuring 7.9 metres (26 feet) in diameter and 94.2 metres (309 feet) tall, growing on a bench on the west side of Carmanah Creek. He recalls taking other cruisers back to the tree the following day to measure it.

Over the next twenty-five years, few people took notice of Gye's claim. A handful of people bushwhacked through the central part of Carmanah Valley, but not one found a tree of such gigantic dimensions.

I first heard about Carmanah's fabled monster in 1980, while pursuing my interest in locating and recording record-sized trees in British Columbia. Letters to government agencies and MacMillan Bloedel produced no new clues. The company's regional forester, Norm Godfrey, checked old cruise records, but found no written indication of an unusually large tree. Further investigations by the company, including conversations with other cruisers on that 1956 trip, failed to substantiate Gye's claim. Carmanah's monster Sitka became as legendary as Paul Bunyan's blue ox.

In the spring of 1981, a crew from Pacific Rim National Park detoured from a routine flight over the West Coast Trail and landed in Carmanah. They reported seeing many magnificent spruce trees, but no Carmanah monster. A year later, Dr. Bristol Foster, then director of the provincial government's ecological reserves unit, invited me to accompany him on a flight into the valley. At that time, Carmanah was still remote, guarded by a large area of unlogged rainforest, so I jumped at the chance.

June 2, 1982, was calm, overcast, and warm. Our helicopter banked steeply over Carmanah Point on the West Coast Trail and headed inland, up the narrow fold of Carmanah Canyon.

Clinton Webb

Randy Stoltmann looks up into the Sitka spruce canopy, twenty storeys above.

As the valley broadened, soaring spruce spires crowded close to the creek bed. We circled tightly down and landed on a gravel bar. For eight hours, five of us walked and thrashed through the untrammelled wild forest. One of the park naturalists noted wolf hair on a twig. Bristol pointed out signs of a more disturbing nature: survey marks which he thought denoted road locations. Although we didn't find the legendary monster spruce, my eyes were opened to the existence of a forest too magnificent to cut down.

I couldn't help but continue to follow the fate of Carmanah.

According to the company's most recently approved plans, its 1985-1989 management and working plan for Tree Farm Licence 44, logging was not scheduled to begin in the big tree groves of mid-Carmanah until the year 2003. But by early 1988, logging roads were already pushing very close. Just how close, no one knew!

On April 1, 1988, Clinton Webb, forest ecologist and a director of Western Canada Wilderness Committee, and I headed toward Carmanah to check out the situation. Clinton piloted wiping the fogged-up windshield with a cotton rag. After a long wet journey on gravel logging roads across Vancouver Island, we entered a spooky, mist-shrouded clearcut, trees still green, lying prone, felled only a few days before. The smell of freshly cut cedar permeated the air.

We parked on an unused spur road. Engine off, the steady drumming of rain on the truck's roof and the drone of a tanker refuelling a grapple yarder a few hundred metres away provided an eerie soundtrack to the dismal scene. Solemnly we readied our packs, donned rain gear, and plunged into the rainforest.

Not twenty minutes later we encountered another logging road. Following it to its end, we re-entered the forest through a tangle of slash. Soon light showed ahead. Minutes later we were picking our way through a clearcut toward a huge pile of logs lining another new road. This second road pushed on, past the idle jaws of an enormous grapple yarder, and ended in virgin forest. Continuing our hike to Carmanah, we were sure that we had left behind the last road.

Bushwhacking along the hillside, we were surprised to see another patch of light below. What appeared at first to be a marsh or some other natural opening turned out to be another freshly cut road. After clambering down the steep side-cut, we began to trudge in deep muck along the bulldozed trail toward Carmanah Valley.

Each turn revealed another fresh incision into the wilderness, bleeding with muddy run-off water. The road-cut continued for some two kilometres (one mile). At its end, ankle-deep in mud, the survey line of plastic ribbons continued down into the heart of Carmanah.

An hour later, after scrambling down to the valley bottom, we stood beneath the dripping boughs of the stately spruce trees at a site that was to become a base for Western Canada Wilderness Committee's crew—Camp Heaven.

That night it rained in a way that would drown anything but a rainforest. In less than twelve hours the creek rose more than sixty centimetres (two feet). It flooded our camp, pitched on the high point of a gravel bar at a place that we thought was well out of reach of the rising water. I could only wonder what the floodwaters would be like if this valley was clear-cut logged.

In the morning we wrung out our sleeping bags, waded off the newly formed island and set off up Carmanah Creek, past great spruce trees scarred by fresh yellow blazes, brightly colored survey tapes, and spraypainted numbers. When Clinton returned a week later, he wandered alone farther upstream into the most magnificent stands of spruce. Here too, the survey marks and the forest service maps confirmed that MacMillan Bloedel had no intention of sparing any part of this forest. Its plans were to log the nation's tallest spruce trees, before the public even knew about them.

We left Carmanah, concerned and uncertain but newly determined to give to the future the opportunity to experience what we had experienced and to learn the secrets of this magical rainforest.

Three spectacular Sitka spruce form cathedral-like spires.

Randy Stoltmann, author of Hiking Guide to the Big Trees of Southwestern British Columbia, *is a director of the Western Canada Wilderness Committee.*

Creation of a Park
Adriane Carr & Paul George

The discoveries made by Randy Stoltmann and Clinton Webb on their weekend trip into Carmanah Valley in the spring of '88 shocked the Western Canada Wilderness Committee. We usually stayed on top of the wilderness scene. Now we faced what seemed to be a losing situation. The logging road was being pushed closer to Carmanah daily. Worse, MacMillan Bloedel (MB), confident that it had sneaked past public scrutiny, selected its first cutting areas in the finest groves of Sitka spruce left standing in Canada, if not in the world.

If we didn't immediately do something extraordinarily effective to counter MB's initiative, by early winter dozens of huge old spruce, 3 metres (10 feet) in diameter and over 78 metres (260 feet) tall, would be felled. Bucked into logs, each tree alone would fill more than an oversized logging truck. Their destiny as raw lumber would leave them indistinguishable from other trees.

Wilderness Committee directors met with Randy and Clinton and emerged with a strategy. We rejected any use of civil disobedience, eschewing such tactics on principle. Clear on what not to do, we met with representatives of the Sierra Club of Western Canada and the Heritage Forests Society of British Columbia. We made a pact to stick together and reject any offer of token preservation by the company. All of us instinctively understood that the integrity of the big trees in Carmanah's valley bottom depended upon the ancient forest thriving on the valley's steep sidehills.

The first step in the campaign to preserve Carmanah was obvious: government decision-makers had to be alerted to the situation. So we helped the Sierra Club of Western Canada and the Heritage Forests Society produce and circulate a thousand copies of a brief entitled, *A Proposal to Add the Carmanah Creek Drainage with Its Exceptional Sitka Spruce Forests to Pacific Rim National Park*. Released on May 13, 1988, this brief featured color photographs contrasting Carmanah's wild beauty with the devastation of nearby clearcuts. Besides calling for "the whole drainage to be preserved," it asked for a two-year moratorium on logging while studies were conducted on the area. By May 19 these efforts had already had an effect. MB decided to voluntarily halt road construction for a one-month study.

Now we needed to tackle the forest industry's propaganda head-on. Since the summer of 1987, and the establishment of South Moresby on the Queen Charlotte Islands as a national park reserve, the industry had been conducting a campaign to convince the public that there was no need for more parks. The industry's ads argued: "Our harvesting is scientifically planned and carried out. . . . Our activities are government approved and completely legitimate. . . . We are providing jobs while replacing the decadent forest with a working forest. . . . We must make room for young healthy trees which will provide jobs and forests forever." One of the industry's TV ads, aired hundreds of times, showed a happy family hiking in a

Centuries to grow; minutes to cut. British Columbia's ancient rainforests are disappearing at an ever-quickening rate.

manicured clearcut. It implied that clearcuts were just as much fun to hike in as were ancient forests.

These would be seductively compelling arguments if it were not for the reality of gigantic ugly clearcuts with wasted wood and eroded soil—clearcuts like those along the last stretch of road to Carmanah. People had to see those clearcuts for themselves. And they had to see Carmanah's giant trees and magical forest. If enough people were exposed to both, we were sure we would win full preservation for the valley.

The Wilderness Committee needed its own video to counteract the industry's propaganda. Unable to afford helicopter access to the valley bottom, we would have to hike the equipment in.

Typical clear-cut logging near Carmanah, where all trees are cut whether they are used or not.

By May 30, a group of soggy Wilderness Committee volunteers was camped in the mud on the new logging road at the edge of Carmanah Valley, ready to start building a trail.

Meanwhile several photographers bushwhacked into the valley. One of them, Adrian Dorst, came back with a photo that was to become the Wilderness Committee's most popular poster of all time, *Carmanah—Big Trees not Big Stumps.*

The small group of committee directors and volunteers began its work in drenching rain, sleeping under plastic tarps on the road in a camp named "Hell." The goal was "Heaven," a spectacular spruce stand in the mid-valley bottom.

Very soon, Hell Camp caught the attention of the logging company. On June 1, coming back to camp after a hard day's trail work, the trail crew met a waiting MB employee who handed Wilderness Committee director George Yearsley a note asking the crew to "cease and desist" building the "trespass trail."

Confident that they were acting within the law, they continued their trail-building activities. Meanwhile, the Wilderness Committee hired a lawyer. On July 22, MB sought a court injunction to stop the trail building. On July 26, the British Columbia Supreme Court rejected the company's application. This ruling established, for the first time in this province, the public's right of access to tree-farm-licensed lands, as long as it did not directly interfere with the licencee's exclusive right to harvest the area's timber.

Within a week the trail was roughed in to Camp Heaven and a video crew hiked into the valley. The trail crew had put in cold, wet, fourteen-hour days to make that access possible.

The trail worked. Not only did it bring in the camera equipment, it also brought in the public. Events quickened. MB announced that it had found the tallest known spruce in the world growing at the bottom of the valley near Pacific Rim park, the 95-metre-tall (312-foot) Carmanah Giant. The company also announced that it would create two small reserves, one of 99 hectares (250 acres) around Heaven Grove, the other only 9 hectares (22 acres) in size around the Carmanah Giant. The company proposed to access both reserves by road—the same logging roads that would lead to clear-cutting the surrounding trees.

The Wilderness Committee thought that its trail system was the answer, so its crew concentrated on building a trail downriver, along the canyon toward the Carmanah Giant. A trail celebration event on the 1988 July long weekend drew two hundred ecstatic people.

Meanwhile, the Wilderness Committee was reaching the wider public with facts about Carmanah like these:

• The entire Carmanah watershed covers only 6,730 hectares (16,825 acres), an area just seventeen times as large as Vancouver's Stanley Park.

• On average, every seventeen days, the equivalent volume of one complete Carmanah Valley's worth of old-growth wood is logged in British Columbia.

• The whole of Carmanah represents less than 2 percent of TFL 44, an amount small enough to be withdrawn by government from the tree farm lands without compensation.

• The valley's forest contains mostly western hemlock and western redcedar, with a relatively small component, just 1.3 percent, of Sitka spruce. Although few in number, Carmanah's Sitka spruce represent Canada's tallest trees and the tallest trees of that species in the world.

"Carmanah fever" was infectious. The valley's big trees and emerald pools caught the imagination of all who saw them. Everyone vowed not to let it become one among hundreds of other British Columbia valleys forested by nature and razed by man as part of the corporate fibre farm. To MB, logging the nation's finest green cathedral was part of the job of a good corporate citizen doing business as usual. To the Wilderness Committee and its hundreds of volunteers, the logging of Carmanah's forest was intensely personal; we were committed to work long hours for as long as it took to save the valley.

As the fight progressed, it was Goliath against David, a company making nearly a million dollars a day in profits against a wilderness preservation movement whose member groups operated with a combined budget of less than one million dollars annually. Both sides rushed to raise public awareness and sell their position. The logging company continued to increase the amount of partial preservation, trying to convince the public that logging should dominate and preservation should be confined to only part of Carmanah's old-growth groves. The preservationists argued that the whole valley must be preserved in order to save the spruce because Carmanah's living system is dynamic. The spongy moss and root wads of the ancient cedars and hemlocks in the upper valley and hillsides are needed to hold back the water and protect and buffer the whole ecosystem. With the entire system intact, giant spruce will grace Carmanah for millenia to come.

The video begun in the first few weeks of the Carmanah campaign was a success. Completed in the fall, it sold thousands of copies. Over a six-month period the Wilderness Committee published three educational newspapers on Carmanah, printing and distributing to the general public a total of 640,000 copies. We published three full-color posters and distributed 150,000 household opinion-poll mailers. We

escorted dignitaries and elected officials and accompanied media and scientists into the valley. We poked huge holes in the company-sponsored research used to rationalize MB's proposal to log 92 percent of Carmanah.

We also continued to extend and improve the trails with the help of hundreds of volunteers. By the end of the summer of 1989, the Carmanah trail system was completed to the top of the valley, linking the entire ecosystem and revealing the importance of the upper valley to the stability of the whole. The Wilderness Committee's trails and guide map enabled thousands of visitors to see Carmanah and created a park that awaited only government recognition.

Trail-builders blaze a route into the valley. Thousands would soon follow.

We had managed to stall the logging for over a year and we had made significant changes in public awareness of the area. When the artists project became a reality, we knew we had a winner. Visual art communicates in a way that statistics and prose never can. The artists could capture the emotional experience shared by all those touched by Carmanah's magic and portray the grandeur which was greater than words. Their visions would surely sway the nation.

Adriane Carr is an instructor of environmental geography. Paul George is a founder of the Western Canada Wilderness Committee. Husband and wife, both are directors of the Wilderness Committee.

This massive, recently felled spruce was already over a century old when Columbus set sail for the Americas.

THE CARMANAH VALLEY

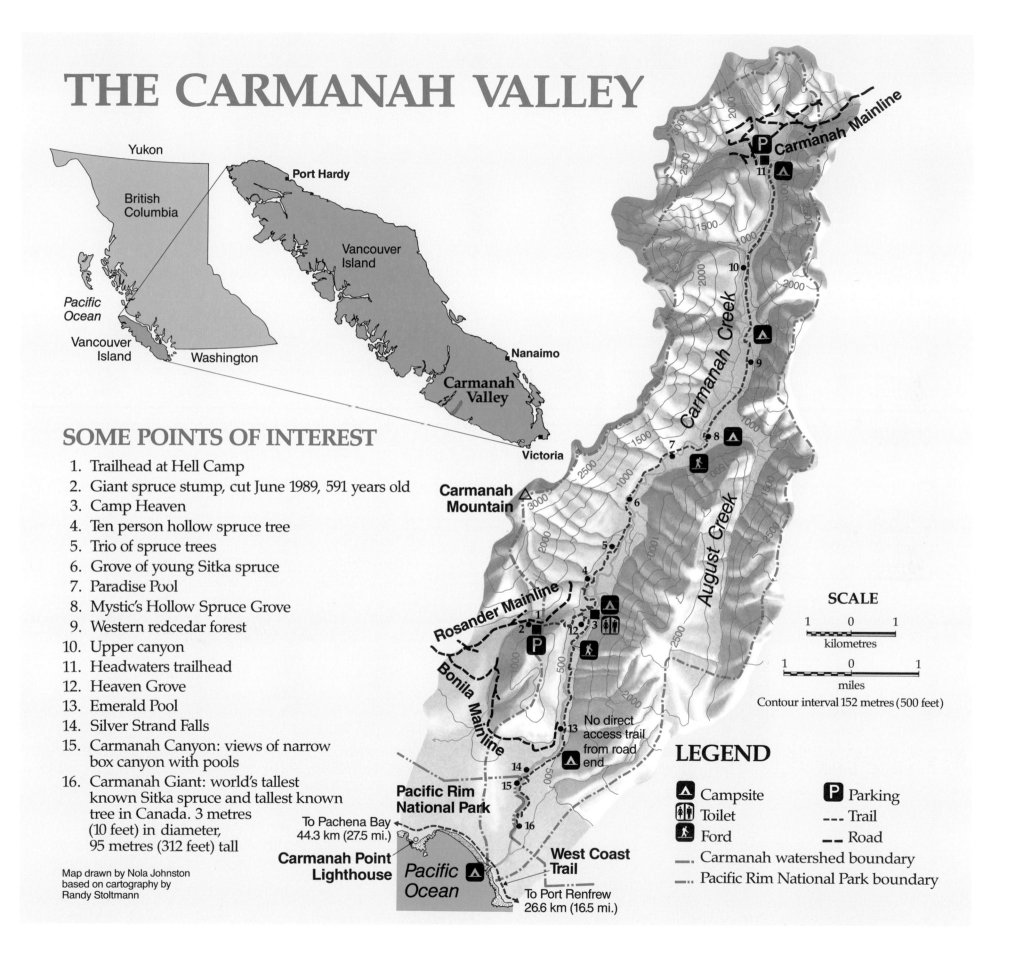

Yukon

British Columbia

Pacific Ocean

Vancouver Island

Washington

Port Hardy

Vancouver Island

Nanaimo

Carmanah Valley

Victoria

SOME POINTS OF INTEREST

1. Trailhead at Hell Camp
2. Giant spruce stump, cut June 1989, 591 years old
3. Camp Heaven
4. Ten person hollow spruce tree
5. Trio of spruce trees
6. Grove of young Sitka spruce
7. Paradise Pool
8. Mystic's Hollow Spruce Grove
9. Western redcedar forest
10. Upper canyon
11. Headwaters trailhead
12. Heaven Grove
13. Emerald Pool
14. Silver Strand Falls
15. Carmanah Canyon: views of narrow box canyon with pools
16. Carmanah Giant: world's tallest known Sitka spruce and tallest known tree in Canada. 3 metres (10 feet) in diameter, 95 metres (312 feet) tall

Map drawn by Nola Johnston
based on cartography by
Randy Stoltmann

Carmanah Mainline

Carmanah Creek

August Creek

Carmanah Mountain

Rosander Mainline

Bonila Mainline

No direct access trail from road end

Pacific Rim National Park

To Pachena Bay 44.3 km (27.5 mi.)

Carmanah Point Lighthouse

Pacific Ocean

West Coast Trail

To Port Renfrew 26.6 km (16.5 mi.)

SCALE

kilometres

miles

Contour interval 152 metres (500 feet)

LEGEND

Campsite   Parking
Toilet   --- Trail
Ford   -- Road
            Carmanah watershed boundary
            Pacific Rim National Park boundary

The Tree-mendous Forest
Sherry Kirkvold

In the fading light, its green, moss-covered base looked like the foot of a giant prehistoric beast. The last rays of sunlight illuminated each limb along the mossy trunk, creating an eerie glow. The tree stood gilt-edged in green light. Its mammoth size defied comprehension.

This giant Sitka spruce (*Picea sitchensis*), one of Canada's tallest trees, has come to symbolize a movement dedicated to preserving some of British Columbia's remaining stands of old-growth forest. Less than one hundred and fifty years of logging on the coast has splintered and fragmented what was once unbroken primeval forest. Ironically, just as we are beginning to realize the complexities of old-growth forests, most of the last stands are scheduled to be logged.

Since the glaciers retreated some ten thousand years ago, climate, topography, geology, and other environmental factors have shaped a tremendously complex ecosystem. Particularly rare, the Sitka spruce system comprises 2 percent of British Columbia's old-growth forest, growing only as a thin fringe along the coast. Rarely reaching more that eighty kilometres inland or elevations of more than three hundred metres, this is the only rainforest species whose

Thread moss (Isothecium) *forms hanging curtains on tree branches.*

Trevor Mills

range is so restricted to the shoreline. Unlike other conifers, Sitka spruce not only tolerates, but actually requires, the magnesium salts contained in ocean spray.

Until recently, the Carmanah Valley remained virtually untouched by human presence. Among the Dididaht (Nitinaht) people who once lived near the mouth of Carmanah Creek, there is an oral tradition of a group of "wild people" who lived somewhere up the valley, but the Dididaht themselves seldom ventured through the narrow canyon that has for so long protected the valley.

Today, Carmanah is reached by a logging road dubbed "Hell Highway," which passes through a recently logged area. With his artist's eye confronted by a landscape of charred stumps, Jim Willer whispered solemnly, "This is like a nightmare in the daytime." Toni Onley compared the devastated clear-cut landscape to the aftermath of the great fire that swept through Dresden after it was bombed.

A trail constructed by Wilderness Committee volunteers descends into the valley. Contrasting sharply with the heat and dust of the road, cool, moist air and luxuriant growth signal the approach to Camp Heaven. At every level, life is vibrant and exuberant: in the soil, in the plants, in the ferns, and in the mosses draping the tree branches.

Many trees are massive columns reaching skyward to heights of up to 95 metres (312 feet) and attaining diameters up to 5.1 metres (16 feet, 8 inches). Immense branches radiate like spokes from the trunks, forming a dense canopy above. Their incredible stature is perhaps only realized when walking the length of a fallen giant. Tangles of salmonberry carpet the floor, along with ferns and mosses. Pink fawn lilies, fairybells, and single delights are among the delicate wildflowers scattered throughout the area. Lacy hemlocks dance gently on the ever-shifting breezes.

In spite of the profuse life, one is struck by a palpable stillness. Between the tap-tapping of the occasional hairy woodpecker,

Pink fawn lilies (Erythronium revolutum) *bloom in early spring.*

the melodious song of winter wrens, and the trills of varied thrushes is an overwhelming silence. Squirrels may be observed, but other small animals such as marten, mice, and voles are easily missed as they travel about. The physical signs of animals such as black-tail deer, cougars, wolves, or bears may be present, but the animals themselves tend to be furtive and well-hidden.

Found only in West Coast forests, the Columbian black-tailed deer is a small subspecies of mule deer.

One of the most exciting discoveries since construction of the trail is a small sea bird, the marbled murrelet, the nesting sites of which were sought by naturalists for a century. Only about fifteen nests have been found world-wide. Despite many efforts, none have yet been located in British Columbia, where it is believed the murrelets nest only in old-growth forests. Sightings of the birds in Carmanah are the first positive proof they use the valley.

Steelhead and cutthroat trout, and chinook and coho salmon spawn in the lower reaches of Carmanah Creek, but these sea-going fish are unable to travel upstream past a series of waterfalls. In the upper reaches of the creek are small resident rainbow trout.

Young Sitka spruce begin life on a recently formed gravel bar.

The spruce groves of the Carmanah floodplain result from a delicate interplay with the meanderings of the stream. As the river shifts its course, gravel bars form in which red alders quickly take root. These trap rich silt coming down the river, providing fertile ground for young Sitka spruce. Alders add nitrogen to the soil and provide an environment in which young spruce can germinate free from major pests. The gravel bars also offer the abundant sunlight required by young spruce.

Extremely fast-growing, young spruce quickly outstrip and replace the alders. Eventually, western hemlock, western red-cedar, and amabilis fir become established among the spruce groves, while hemlock, amabilis fir, and yellow-cedar grow on the surrounding hillsides. Hemlock, which tolerates deep shade, often grows slowly until the creation of a sunny opening allows it to grow more quickly. One hemlock stump in an adjacent valley was dated and found to be three hundred years old, even though its diameter was only twenty-five centimetres (ten inches)!

If the trees are logged off the hillsides, thereby removing water-retaining vegetation, it is uncertain what will happen to the water levels in the stream. If the peak flow increases, it could destroy the gravel bars on which young spruce begin their lives as well as erode the existing giants. Alders would continue to take over newly opened areas, but the young spruce would not tolerate the flooding. Without young spruce trees, these forest groves would eventually be supplanted by hemlock.

The spruce trees grow to such immense heights that their bases are in one set of climatic conditions, their trunks in a second, and the crowns in a third. These layers, or zones, are part of the structure of this forest. High up in the top layer, dominated by spruce and a few tall hemlocks, tiny needles carry out the task of photosynthesis, the basis for all life. In the middle zone, shorter trees are laden with moss. The ground storey is the most diverse, tenanted by a profusion of young trees, berry bushes, herbs, ferns, and mosses.

Fallen salmonberry petals (Rubus spectabilis) *add a touch of color.*

It should amaze us that our temperate rainforests can attain such colossal stature. They are frequently scourged by winter storms; the soils are thin; and for half the year the sun shines, but there is little rain, while for the other half, roughly three metres (ten feet) of rain fall and the sun seldom shines. In spite of these conditions, these forests attain a biomass (weight of plants per hectare) of nearly twice that of a tropical rainforest.

The Carmanah spruce groves occur in a particularly generous habitat. The surrounding hillsides provide shelter for the shallow-rooted trees, and the creek has deposited fertile soil. The growing conditions are so favorable that five-hundred-year-old spruce trees along the river are much taller than cedars that have grown on the surrounding hillsides for a thousand years.

Spruce, like other conifers, develop mutually beneficial relationships between their root tips and certain funguses, known as mycorrhizae. The fungus absorbs minerals, nitrogen, and water from the soil, and provides them to the tree. In exchange, the tree supplies sugars that the chlorophyll-lacking

The beautiful but deadly amanita (Amanita muscaria) *decomposes litter on the forest floor.*

fungus is unable to manufacture. Squirrels, mice, voles, and certain insects eat the fruiting bodies of the funguses, then carry the spores in their intestines to new sites. Because many of these funguses are truffles, which live entirely underground, they have no other method of dispersal. Small

Bracket funguses break down the wood of dead trees.

20

mammals are thus a vital component of a healthy forest.

It takes more than just old trees to make an old-growth forest. An old-growth forest is one that has developed a mix of species, sizes, and ages. As canopy trees die, they provide the snags, stumps, and logs that are habitat for many species of wildlife. Decay is very much a part of the process of life in the forest. Particularly numerous in temperate rainforests, billions of decay organisms interact in every cubic metre of soil.

A tree that has lived for eight hundred years may continue to serve the forest for another five hundred years after its death. Initially, micro-organisms begin to soften the wood. Bark beetles chew their way in, introducing fungal spores and bacteria. Mites, termites, carpenter ants, and others join the feast. If the tree remains standing, woodpeckers begin hunting the insect hordes inside. The cavities they carve become nesting sites for a variety of forest birds, bats, and other cavity users.

When the tree falls, plants such as western hemlock and huckleberry begin to root in the wood. All these activities release the nutrients stored in the tree during its life. Every bit of these "nurse logs" is made available to plants and animals in forms they can use. Everything is recycled; nothing is wasted.

This dynamic ecosystem has developed over thousands of years. It functions perfectly. One thing is certain: if the forest is logged, the new forest that grows up will not be the same as this forest. If even part of the valley is logged, the spruce may be exposed to the wind and blown over. The secret to growing the world's tallest spruce trees could be lost forever.

The old wood of this stump is recycled as it nourishes new growth.

This forest radiates wholeness, stability, and calm, though it is ever-changing. It gives a sense of solidity and strength. Yet it is vulnerable, for in a blink of time, these trees can be felled—these trees that have witnessed so much.

Those who have visited Carmanah have found a place from which to draw strength and be renewed. It is a place of refreshment. It is also important for its scientific value—it is a gene bank for the future. A small remnant of a vanishing ancient forest, it is a place worth fighting for.

Weekdays, the roar and whine of logging equipment sound around the rim of the watershed. The artists who have come to Carmanah hope to keep them at bay; they have voiced their opinion through their art. Society must hear their voices and make critical decisions. We have but one chance to make a decision to protect this area. That chance is now.

Sherry Kirkvold is a naturalist and environmental educator who has been involved in forest issues both locally and in Africa.

21

One Hundred Artists
Arne Hansen

Once in a while the Western Canada Wilderness Committee stumbles on innovative new ways to save wild areas. One such effort is the immensely successful Carmanah expedition, the result of a two-year alliance with well-known West Coast artists.

We joined forces in 1987, when this writer discussed with artist Toni Onley the Wilderness Committee's difficulty in raising funds. That meeting resulted in our printing five thousand fine art reproductions of three of Toni's watercolors. A few months later he suggested we fly a dozen of British Columbia's top landscape artists to Stein Lake, auction off the resulting works, and produce an art book about the event.

The Stein Valley book didn't happen because we could neither afford it nor did we have the staff to organize such a massive publishing effort. One year made all the difference. By the spring of '89, when the Carmanah expedition was well along in its planning stages, Ken Budd appeared in our office. We listened attentively as he showed us his past publishing successes and spun a picture of creative financing which made it possible to consider such a huge project. We were sold.

Meanwhile, in Tofino, artist and committee organizer Mark Hobson had been working quietly on the Carmanah project at his studio. He had invited about seventy artists from Vancouver Island plus our faithful 1988 Stein participants. We had originally expected to take about forty artists to Carmanah because Mark had estimated that at least half of his invitations would be turned down. Few declined and by April more than one hundred artists had signed up to support the Carmanah project.

Back on the mainland, word of our plans had spread and the Wilderness Committee office was flooded with phone calls from numerous artists who wanted to come along. Panic was about to set in, so we closed the list. As it was, our largest expedition of thirty-five artists in June grew to ninety-three people by the time camp crew, cooks, reporters, photographers, one film and three TV crews arrived. Our amazing

kitchen volunteers came through in the pinch and dealt expertly with the friendly mob.

Mother Nature cooperated as well. Carmanah is a rainforest, yet we had perfect weather every time we brought artists to the valley during the four expeditions we mounted between May and August.

An artists' village sprouted beside Carmanah Creek on a gravel bar known as Camp Heaven.

It was always exciting to watch three or four vans plus assorted cars and trucks arrive at the trailhead, and to see everyone load up and head down the valley systematically. We felt a lot like Barnum and Bailey at times, except this crowd, the artists, kept cheering us on long into the night.

Many of these visual masters said it was the highlight of their careers to go to Carmanah, be involved in the politically charged debate, and experience the majesty and mystique of the valley.

Carmanah was also a dilemma for the artists, many of whom were used to painting the beauty of nature. Most came in by road, where they were struck by the devastation of clearcuts. Even after arriving in the pristine lower valley, they were bombarded by the roar and grind of logging machinery in nearby watersheds.

During breakfast, dinner, and on into the late evening, discussion centred around the issue of clear-cutting our remaining old-growth forests, its political implications, and prospects for the future of wilderness in the province.

One message from the artists was clearly received by the committee: "Thank you for letting us speak." Many had been working on the issue individually, but when invited to sign up for this expedition they jumped at the chance to join forces. A united voice on environmental issues can accomplish so much more, they said. Several stated that if the Group of Seven artists were alive today, they would all be in the forefront of the struggle to protect our wild places.

The outrage expressed by the artists focused on the fact that they enjoy painting and drawing natural settings that people can visit. They don't want to become chroniclers of places of beauty that once existed.

Historically, visual artists have always held a mirror up to society, making social comment through their art work. British Columbia artists Robert Bateman, Donald Curley, Toni Onley, Bill Reid, Takao Tanabe, and Jim Willer contributed to *Islands at the Edge*, a book that played an important part in the creation of South Moresby national park reserve.

Most people realize that the Stein, Carmanah Valley, Clayoquot Sound, and the many parts of British Columbia being fought for by environmentalists are only symptoms of a much larger problem: a gluttonous, out-of-control forest industry.

Kevin Oke

Carmanah, Camp Heaven, and a cozy fire create camaraderie.

Musicians, writers, film makers, and a host of other creative people are jumping into the fray. With their help and with growing public awareness, the cycle of greed and devastation can be halted. One day we will no longer be called on to quantify nature and put a dollar value on ancient trees, mountains, and wildlife.

Mark Hobson

An army of volunteers prepared meals for the artists. Everyone pitched in to help clean up.

Journalist Arne Hansen is a director of the Western Canada Wilderness Committee and has acted as the coordinator for this project.

Randy Anderson

Born in 1958, in Edmonton, Alberta, Randy Anderson studied art at Douglas College in Surrey, British Columbia; Concordia University in Montreal, Quebec; and the Emily Carr College of Art and Design in Vancouver, British Columbia. He works primarily in the areas of installation and performance art but has always used drawing as an important part of a work's development. The content of his work deals with the dehumanizing effects of our consumer society.

Anderson has worked with Greenpeace on a number of issues, including disarmament and toxic waste. A resident of Vancouver, he is currently one of the directors of the Western Front and is the founding director of a non-profit exhibition space called Gallery T.O.O. Anderson's work has been shown in Canada, the United States, and Europe.

The drive into Carmanah is an experience not to be missed. It's called bearing witness. Once a person has seen the logging practices first hand, I can't imagine not wanting to stop it. Of course, it can't be stopped completely. The forest industry is part of the economic backbone of this province. And there lies the reason to change the way logging is done, so that it is a sustainable industry, conscious of its impact on our environment. Carmanah Valley is little to ask for, considering the damage already done.

Carmanah should be spared the chainsaw. There is no doubt about it. The problem is that it shouldn't have to be "saved" at all! People in other countries envy the richness of our natural heritage and are appalled at how we handle it. It all comes down to money, as it does elsewhere in the world, but we haven't learned from those mistakes and continue a record of mismanagement and short-sightedness.

The priorities of our society are all wrong. Let's save the valley—then let's change the economic structure of this country so that valleys don't have to be "saved" in the future. They will be left to enrich our lives and the lives of future generations.

I've chosen not to describe my drawing. Individuals viewing the piece will react to it in their own ways, depending on their frames of reference. That is what I want— an emotional reaction as well as an analytical response.

When a Tree Falls
charcoal on paper
127 X 97 cm (50" X 38¼")

Judith M. Atkinson

Judith Atkinson has always found art-making to be a place of exploration, ideas, tactile expression, and quiet contemplation; by age eleven, she had decided to be an artist. Her work has been influenced by Monet, Degas, Matisse, Emily Carr, Van Gogh, J.W. Morrice, Jack Shadbolt, Charles Gagnon, Nancy Graves, Richard Diebenkorn, Robert Motherwell, Irene Whithome, and Tapies.

She is moved by the elemental in her work, whether it is the notion of spiritual transcendence or the pure joy of color and movement in the landscape. She involves herself with different themes using varying degrees of abstraction. She has worked in two and three dimensions: drawing, painting, pastel, mixed media sculpture, plaster pieces, and clay. Her work ranges in scale from wall drawings measuring thirty metres (one hundred feet) on each side, to small eight-centimetre-square (three-inch) icon paintings.

Her heart aches when a large old tree passes by on a logging truck, and she weeps at the bleak nothingness of the clearcut, just centimetres before the lush Carmanah rainforest. As an artist, she believes in doing what she can, as did Monet, who saved the beautiful poplars he was painting by buying the farmer's field. She hopes that by painting the beauty of this forest, it will not vanish.

*E**verything is green. Everything thing is waiting and still. Slowly things begin to move, to slip their places. Groups and masses and lines tie themselves together. Colors you had not noticed come out, timidly or boldly. In and out your eye passes. Nothing is crowded; there is living space for all. Air moves between each leaf. Sunlight plays and dances. Nothing is still now. Life is sweeping through the spaces. Everything is alive. The air is alive. The silence is full of sound. The green is full of color. Light and dark chase each other. Here is a picture, a complete thought, and there another and there. . . There are themes everywhere, something sublime, something ridiculous, or joyous, or calm, or mysterious. Tender youthfulness laughing at gnarled oldness. Moss and ferns, and leaves and twigs, light and air, depth and color chattering. . . you must be still in order to hear and see.***

Emily Carr, *Hundreds and Thousands*
(Clarke, Irwin, and Company Ltd., 1966)

These words of Emily Carr echo my experience of the Carmanah Valley—the stillness, the solitude, the green, the magic. Everything is teeming with life and joy—from the fern turning to the sun, the swirling pattern of cedar bark, to the majesty of the giants. It is truly a symphony of green, with every imaginable variation on the palette. There is the delight of discovering the beautiful cadmium-red roots of the cedar, the soft yellow-green of the angel hair moss, and the rich brown earth. I was also struck by the sense of movement—of light, pattern, and energy from moment to moment.

Referring to the ancient giant forests of the Queen Charlotte Islands, Bill Reid speaks of the "almost forgotten value, the aesthetic value, the nurture it affords human life." We must look at the renewal, restoration, and regeneration that the forest provides for us on every human level and tie into the Gaia principle as we approach the twentieth century. My descent into the valley took longer than most travelers, as I was continuously struck by a sense of wonder at the magic of the Carmanah.

J. M. Atkinson.

Giant of the Carmanah Rainforest
pastel
51 X 66 cm (20" X 26")

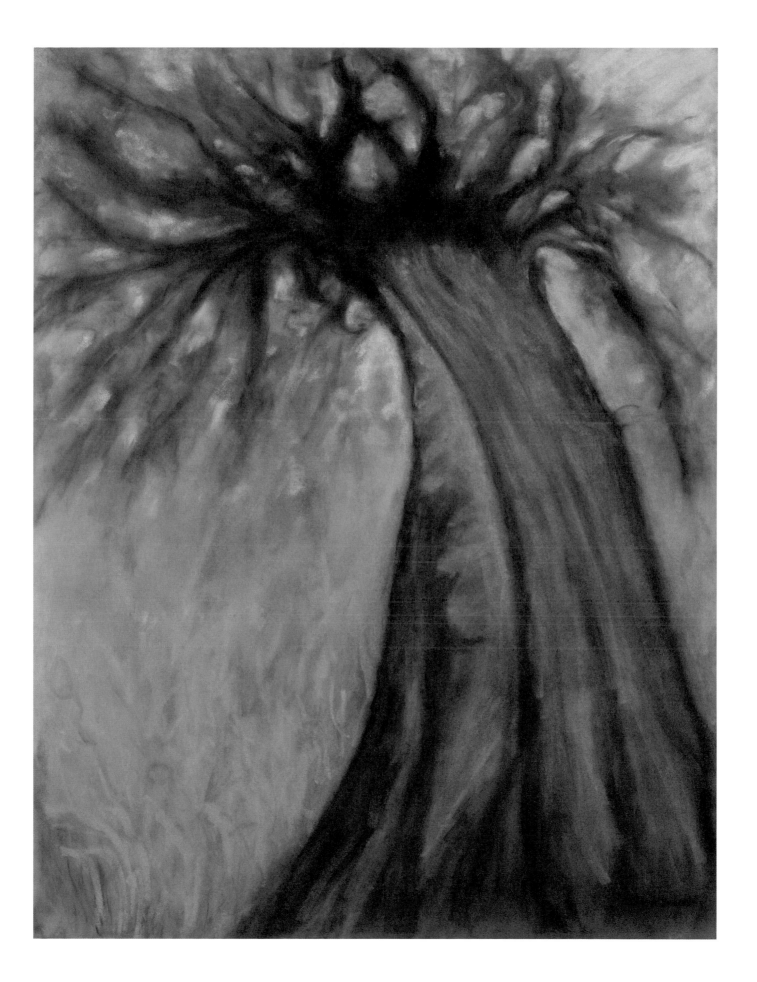

Robert Bateman

Born in Toronto, Ontario, Robert Bateman was a keen artist and naturalist from his early days. He has painted using a variety of styles, but in the early sixties, he began to develop the realistic style that has made him one of the foremost artists depicting the world of nature.

Bateman has a degree in geography from the University of Toronto, and his art reflects his commitments to ecology and preservation. A spokesman for many environmental and preservation issues, he has used his artwork and limited edition reproductions in fund-raising efforts which have provided millions of dollars for worthy causes.

Bateman has had numerous sell-out exhibitions in Canada, the United States, and Great Britain. His work is in many public and private collections, including several art museums. He was commissioned by the Governor General of Canada to do a painting as the wedding gift for HRH Prince Charles from the people of Canada. He has had many one-man museum shows throughout North America, including the Smithsonian Institute in Washington, D. C. He was made an officer of the Order of Canada, and has received numerous awards, honors, and honorary doctorates. He has also been the subject of three films. Two books of his art, The Art of Robert Bateman *and* The World of Robert Bateman, *have sold more than half a million copies.*

It has always been a quest for me, to see great, old-growth forests; of them all, I like the Carmanah Valley the best. This seems to be the most accessible. You have to really work hard in the others to get any kind of vista. Here, there's an openness and a scale and a character that is easy for the mind to grasp. Now remains the challenge, "Can I paint it?" Capturing the imagery in this kind of forest is the most difficult in the whole natural world as far as I'm concerned.

To get here, we came through vast clear-cut areas. They were shocking to me as someone who cares not only about forests but the way they've been cut down. The waste is particularly shocking. It's ridiculous to call what we want, single use and what the logging companies want, multiple use. This can be multiple use for all kinds of people who want to use and enjoy it, from scientists right down to little children. Once they've had their way with it, it will be just like thousands of hectares of the rest of British Columbia —nothing special. It's special right now.

Meaningful work for human beings is important, but for logging companies to use a forest like this as job blackmail is ridiculous. People's livelihoods are really being threatened by the practices of the British Columbia government and the big logging companies. We should be doing things about mechanization, about more labor-intensive, small-scale logging, and particularly about more aggressive marketing of lumber and finished wood products instead of exporting raw logs. Before we start scraping the bottom of the barrel, we should start tightening our belts and changing our ways.

The line has to be drawn somewhere and something as precious and unique as this is where the line should be drawn. I ask the question, "Are our current forest practices because of good management and stewardship or are they due to ignorance, laziness and greed?" That's a question I think the people of British Columbia and the people of Canada should be asking. I'm afraid the answer is all too evident.

Robert Bateman

Carmanah Contrasts
acrylic on board, a dyptych
102 X 114 cm (40" X 45")

Thomas Beck

Thomas Beck grew up in the midwestern United States during the fifties and sixties. At an early age, he collected wasp nests, leaves, feathers, and rocks, fascinated by their colors, shapes, and textures. He found that drawing them came naturally to him—a gift from his father. He became a technical illustrator, but in his early twenties at Ohio State University, he discovered his ability to paint, and straight lines and perfect curves are passing out of his life as his career shifts.

Beck's first subjects were animals. Animal portraits and studies soon matured into environmentally integrated compositions. After moving to Seattle in 1980, he began experimenting with different mediums. Oils and pen and ink gave way to watercolors, which best suited his style. His involvement in environmental issues provided new impetus for his work. Endangered species are now the primary subjects of his paintings. The step-by-step process of following his heart has resulted in a deep level of artistic self-expression.

I am honored to be the sole artist from the United States invited to participate in the Carmanah campaign. I hope we can improve communication between environmentalists in Canada and in the United States so we can help each other and learn from one another.

I am an environmental artist specializing in paintings of endangered animals and habitats. I believe strongly in the sanctity of all life. Wild animals possess a dignity, beauty, and individuality that can only be fully appreciated when they are in their natural environment. My work is a connecting link between nature and those of us who have lost touch with the Earth. I am thus a catalyst for inciting in people a renewed love of nature and a desire to preserve this delicate planet. Without such renewed vision, the sequoia forests, humpback whales, and Carmanahs of this world will pass away and our children will weep for them.

My greatest hope is that, through my work, people will become aware of the environmental challenges we impose upon ourselves. Humans are stewards of the earth. As such, it is our privilege to ensure that wild animals are allowed to fulfill their birthright: to continue their own kind in a natural, unspoiled world. Ultimately, humankind will share the same fate that we impose upon wildlife and wild places.

Carmanah has a very spiritual value for me. I feel the presence of God here. When I watch the stars at night, I know that heaven is on Earth. Camp Heaven, that's where we are.

Our greatest gift would be to give back to nature more than we take from it.

Small Blessings
watercolor and gouache on paper
30 X 35 cm (12" X 13½")

THOMAS BECK
©1989

Susanna Blunt

Susanna Blunt decided she wanted to be an artist when she was three years old, and she never changed her mind.

As a teenager she spent three summers at the Banff Centre School of Fine Arts and after finishing high school, she went to England where she lived for the next nine years.

She studied at the Byam Shaw School of Drawing and Painting in London for three years and graduated in 1962. She won a scholarship to the Royal Academy where she studied for a further four years and was awarded several scholarships and medals for landscapes and portraits during that time.

During her last year in England, she worked for Yoko Ono, assisting her with several art projects. In 1968, she moved to San Francisco and taught at the College of Marin.

She has lived in Vancouver since 1970, painting portraits, murals, and landscapes. She has taught many private and public classes including three years at the University of British Columbia in the fine arts department and at the centre for continuing education.

Blunt has exhibited in Canada, the United States, England, and Italy, and has done commissions for people in many other countries as well, including Scotland, Ireland, Holland, Belgium, France, Germany, Australia, Japan, the Philippines, and in Hong Kong.

I once flew with Toni Onley in his plane to California. I cried all the way there and all the way back and he never took me anywhere again.

My trip to the Carmanah, where I went with my husband and eight-year-old son, reminds me of this, and I'm afraid they might never take me anywhere again either.

Now, while it is true that I am quite cowardly about many things—flying, bears (I did not dare camp in the Carmanah with the other, braver artists)—I am, on the other hand, exceedingly stubborn.

Earlier this summer, I fell over the only small stone on an otherwise smooth and untroubled path in West Vancouver. A ridiculous number of injuries resulted from this fall, but I decided in my profound ignorance (never having hiked anywhere in my life) to go to the Carmanah as planned.

I bandaged one wrenched ankle and put the other with its torn ligaments into an aircast. I bandaged my hand with its sprained thumb and ignored my wrenched shoulder. I also ignored the grim look in my husband's eye as he packed the car.

Many hours later, we stood gazing into the forest at a sea of black mud and twisted roots, only just visible through the dense cloud of mosquitoes. I confess now that my heart sank like the proverbial stone. The mosquitoes descended en masse onto my head and savagely bit my scalp for the next five hours.

It got much steeper, much harder, and I discovered later that when my husband was not either supporting me down or hauling me up, he was taking pictures of me.

Despite the relentless stream of insults directed at me by my impatient and unsympathetic child, and the amazed or ribald comments of passing fellow hikers, and in spite of myself, we made it!

Since I didn't see anything above foot level, here is my painting of what I saw.

My husband, true hero of this story, suggests I call it *Stumble*. Thank you, dear husband, for having so kindly helped me, and long live the Carmanah Valley!

Susanna P. Blunt

Carmanah Valley
oil on canvas
41 X 51 cm (16" X 20")

Ross Bollerup

Ross Bollerup's interest in landscape images began early in his career and continues with the Carmanah experience. He believes humanity is unavoidably part of the natural world and is presently exploring the many facets of this relationship in his work. At home in Rosedale, British Columbia, by Mt. Cheam, he lives with his wife, a biologist who shares his interests. They have two children. Bollerup paints images of his garden and the small animals and other creatures that live on their property, as well as the surrounding mountains, highways, rivers, buildings, and waterfalls.

He has been teaching part time since 1969 and has worked with a wide cross-section of students, from those who were advanced in their disciplines, to those just beginning.

His first important exhibition was at the Bau-Xi Gallery in 1966. Since then, he has exhibited extensively throughout the Lower Mainland, as well as the rest of British Columbia. The Contemporary Art Gallery and the Mary Frazee Art Gallery, as well as the Burnaby, Surrey, Prince George, Victoria, and Vancouver art galleries have all exhibited his work. He has also shown in smaller galleries in Chilliwack, Harrison Hot Springs, Mission, and Grand Forks; and he has participated occasionally in group shows in various centres across Canada and the United States.

Carmanah Valley is a place that should be preserved, not only for its material value but also for its spiritual value. This spirituality is evident in the beauty of the trees and in the way this forest is organized in its natural way—truly a gift. This is a place from which we can learn more and more—both now and as our consciousness, understanding, and awareness increase. For these reasons alone, this remarkable area should be preserved as a treasure and kept safe for future generations.

The majesty and naturalness of Carmanah Valley are very inspiring. It is fuel for my creativity, it is grist for the mill. I can see images here that I've been working on in the past because there is a continuity in the ideas behind my work and a continuity in the way nature works.

When I'm out there in the forest, I'm making my paintings, but I'm also referring in my memory to past painting experiences. I'm making new discoveries about how beauty is put together, discoveries that will emerge again in future work. This is how the Carmanah project contributes to the ongoing cycle of image experiences.

My time in Carmanah was a great artistic experience for me; I enjoyed it immensely. It has been educational to be with a group that is outstanding in my eyes, both as artists and as people who are concerned about the natural world and want to understand more about it. Humanity is at a stage where this understanding is vital to our survival. The Carmanah project has given me new insight into the value of our great forests and of nature in general. My goal now is to reveal the spiritual reality that I sense in the Carmanah Valley and to try to express that reality in my art—not only for myself, but for others as well.

Ross Bollerup

Carmanah Remembers
monotype on rag paper
91 X 61 cm (36" X 24")

Elizabeth Bromley

Elizabeth Bromley began her art studies at the Vancouver School of Art (now the Emily Carr College of Art and Design). She has continued to study with various instructors, and most recently at the University of British Columbia. Her interest in art has taken her on painting trips to Florence, Italy, and to the Auvergne and Burgundy regions of France.

Her art has evolved through the trends of the fifties and sixties, such as abstraction and non-objective painting, and now she just enjoys a "painterly" style of painting. She sometimes works in watercolors, but prefers the impasto and the strength of oils. She is a resident of Vancouver.

Much of the drive into the Carmanah was as if we were moving through a war-torn country, clear-cut logging being the culprit. It did, however, make entering the Carmanah Trail all the more awesome.

As I picked my way down into the valley, the only word that would come to me was, "Wow!"—and this utterance came frequently. It was not a great intellectual word, admittedly, but it was a natural expression of my feelings. The beauty of Carmanah is indeed almost beyond words.

I can only say that in my few days there, spent in the tranquility and splendor of that forest while I sketched and painted, I felt total contentment and happiness. It was an experience I shall never forget.

Those feelings, though, are shared with an undercurrent of sadness: a totally incredible thought that someone, somewhere, could give the order to destroy this fascinating sanctuary and its living monuments forever.

I feel that this natural heritage of magnificent spruce trees should be protected and cherished, to be enjoyed by future generations.

Surely this is not too much to ask. With our affluence, can we not afford to save this special place?

If this protection is not forthcoming, we lose more than just landscape; we lose something of ourselves.

Elizabeth Bromley.

Forest Fantasia
oil on canvas
61 x 61 cm (24" x 24")

Alan J. Bruce

Alan J. Bruce was born in Saskatchewan in 1935 and moved to Victoria, British Columbia, in 1965.

In Victoria, the watercolor work of Stephen Lowe captivated Bruce's mind, as did the subtleties of nature on Vancouver Island. He studied with Stephen Lowe as well as with Stephanie Q. Steele, both of whom provided impetus for his pursuit of the medium.

Bruce was accepted as an associate of the Federation of Canadian Artists in 1981 and as a signature member of the Northwest Watercolor Society in 1986. His paintings often combine the Eastern aesthetic of simplicity with Western design and color, resulting in a unique capturing of nature and wood.

His paintings have been shown in numerous exhibits and traveling shows. His work hangs in many private collections in Canada and the United States and is currently represented by Image Makers Gallery, or Winchester Galleries, Victoria, British Columbia.

The garments of the mother have been ripped and torn, and society as a whole is now being forced to re-evaluate its position and its own effect on the elements of nature.

The delicate balance in which our ecosystem survives has become the mirror of the consciousness of mankind—and the signs indicate that drastic changes are needed, and have been needed for some time. The time has arrived when nature could continue to give freely, but man has abused that bounty. He has not recognized within himself his affinity with the forces of nature.

Mother Nature has provided greatly for our needs, and for those individuals whose veils have been lifted, she also provides no end of nourishment—both aesthetic and primal. But we have not respected these gifts and taken care not to destroy their source.

Most certainly we require the physical goods nature provides, but the governing forces have seemingly not understood that nature—not man—is the provider of these goods.

As a multitude of problems arises from our modern-day society, it must surely become obvious that there must be a better way—not only to log the forests, but to view nature in general.

The industrial economy to which man is tethered has, in many ways, left us blinded to what lies down the road. Surely common sense will tell us that there will be no jobs when there are no forests; surely common sense will tell us that it is not possible to replant and replace, to reap a duplicate of what we once had. There will always be something amiss.

Trying to attune nature to a man-created environment is akin to putting on a synthetic garment. It may work for awhile, but the natural world will not forever be able to regenerate, leaving us far from what we had originally, leaving us with a shifting wildlife populace and land which will be undermined and unable to sustain what once was.

Please look and understand.

A Symbol of the Roots of Our Heritage
watercolor
70 x 51 cm (27³/₄" x 20")

Drew Burnham

Drew Burnham was born in Kamloops, British Columbia, in 1947. After growing up in smaller communities around the province, he attended university in Victoria, completing two years of the fine arts program under the eyes of Toni Onley and John Dobereiner.

A trip to Europe in 1969, at the expense of his Harley Davidson, gave him an opportunity to undertake intense personal studies in art galleries; sometimes he spent days looking at the same painting. Success followed closely with the figurative and very expressive oils he developed at the University of Victoria, and by 1970 he moved to Vancouver and the Vancouver School of Art (now the Emily Carr College of Art and Design), this time traveling on an ancient Royal Enfield motorcycle with an off-round wheel. The resulting philosophic collision with abstraction is still reverberating in his studio, having pushed him through diverse and conflicting directions over the ensuing fifteen years—first distilling into an integrated series, then fragmenting into further searching, in the process yielding some intriguing bodies of work and awards in Canada and the United States.

Presently Burnham is exhibiting the more playful of his series, done in watercolor and acrylics using bits of houses, shrubs, and trees as subject material. His work is currently well represented in the Lower Mainland, Vancouver Island, the Okanagan Valley, Alberta, and Washington State.

I like the feeling of being in places like this, where you get an ageless, timeless, quiet feeling. I believe some of these areas should be left as they are. The experience of this forest gives you an idea of age and a feeling that things do live for a long time. A second-growth forest doesn't have the same depth of spiritual quality that exists among these big trees.

When I was growing up, I went through a period of turmoil. A major stabilizing thing at that time was seeing a fir tree during a horrible stormy night. It was windy and rainy and cold, and this tree was standing there through it all. Birds landed in it and the wind blew and it stood there unaffected. I thought, "Anything can happen and this tree just keeps standing there. It doesn't sweat; it doesn't worry; it probably doesn't have any stress. Why can't a person be that way?" Trees have become my symbol of stability, longevity, and even sanity—the plain sanity of surviving.

The Carmanah forest brings about a calm. Being here tends to clarify my ability to think in visual concepts. I find it very much a right climate to work in. All humans, whether they come here or not, have the potential to experience a forest like this. But it is something they will not get if they don't come to it and certainly will not ever get a chance to have if the forest isn't here. It is not fair that a place like this gets taken out just so that a few people can have some money in their pockets. It is just plain not worth it.

Thought Bush for Carmanah
Panel three of four
acrylic and oil on canvas
92 x 102 cm (36″ x 40″)

Lissa Calvert

Lissa Calvert has been painting and drawing wildlife from an early age. At seventeen she was illustrating books for well-known outdoor adventure writer Michael Cramond. Later she illustrated many books for major Canadian publishers. She was also commissioned to design a series of plates and figurines for the world-famous Goebel of Germany. While developing her career as an artist, Calvert worked as an art director for film and television. Imperial Oil toured her Arctic Wildlife *show to museums and public galleries from coast to coast. She has traveled extensively in North America to broaden her knowledge of its animals.*

Her wildlife painting is a logical development of a fascination with nature that began in childhood. She regularly travels into "the bush" to see animals in their natural habitat. That vivid mental image of the animal in its own space and environment, a separate nation, is integral to her painting. The quest for authenticity, knowledge, and feeling is part of her lifelong professional endeavor to paint the natural world in all its complexity and magic.

In a general sense Carmanah is not extraordinary. An extra ten metres (thirty-three feet) at the top of the spruce in this valley is irrelevant on a coast typified by tall trees. What is extraordinary is that we can have reached a situation where, if nothing is done, out of the hundreds of valleys similar to Carmanah on our coast, only a tiny handful will remain. They are vanishing fast. No one really imagined that the whole west coast of this island could be stripped during this century, but it looks like it's going to happen very soon.

What an indictment, here on a continent where Sequoia National Park was set aside in 1890, Banff in 1887, and Yellowstone in 1872.

An issue that has become very polarized lately is that of people's jobs versus preservation of these pieces of forest. There is an idea that trees are essentially here to produce fuel and houses and newspapers and furniture. In a sense they are, but their primary function is to be an oxygen pump and a carbon dioxide fixer and to keep our very fragile environment for the whole planet within the range that sustains life. The process of cutting down rainforests in the tropics and northern zones is extremely dangerous. This issue is a lot bigger than houses and jobs. To talk of jobs being lost is like worrying about missing breakfast while the *Titanic* is sinking. The grandchildren of those people aren't going to be alive if we keep doing this.

Fortunately the Carmanah is heartbreakingly beautiful. Perhaps, by using this drawing power, we can help to save it.

As old-growth forest does not support large deer populations, wolves are rare in Carmanah, but they use the trails and creeks as hunting corridors. Wolves have always been symbols of life and death, themes never far from consciousness here, with the towering, extravagant flora and baroque, honey-combed, fallen trees.

Crossing the Carmanah—Timber Wolves
acrylic on board
107 x 66 cm (42" x 26")

Simon H. Camping

Simon Camping was born in Dokkum, the Netherlands, in 1928. He came to Canada in 1954 and settled in Calgary, Alberta. Since 1981, he has lived on Saltspring Island in British Columbia.

Camping is a self-taught artist who works in watercolors. He has had many one-man shows throughout Western Canada and is represented in numerous corporate and private collections in Europe, Canada, and the United States.

His paintings reflect a reverent attitude toward the beauty and power of nature: "The unspoiled wildness of nature is a reflection of the One who created it. The wonder of life—the brilliance of color, the violence of a storm, the starkness of winter, the solitude—is a religious experience made visible and touchable."

Painting this beauty in wildness is an extension of frequent trips between the sea and the mountains.

My family was very much after me to go to Carmanah, especially my twenty-three-year-old daughter. It's been a wonderful experience. Everyone I talk to is very enthusiastic and has a concern for this valley—that somehow, let's try to save it. It's a great feeling, too, that maybe we're helping a little bit.

This is an area I'm not very familiar with in my painting. If I paint forests it's usually from the outside, rather than from the inside. Most of my paintings are of the mountains. This is an entirely different environment with an entirely different feeling to it. Mountains are big, but they're big in a different way.

Age has a lot to do with this forest. In a sense, there is something slightly menacing, slightly foreboding here. I love trees, but these are more than trees. They are huge. They make you feel very insignificant and very reverent. I'm a Christian and that goes through your whole life, especially in a place like this. It's like being in a huge cathedral. I have very much a feeling of worship, being here. I guess that's why it's so important to keep places like this big enough so that they can keep on living, rather than having a little bunch of big trees with everything cut down around it.

A lot of these places shouldn't really be developed at all. I've seen so many places that are very beautiful become tourist attractions. Once all the tourist facilities are installed, in no time at all they're crawling with people. Of course, if you talk and think like that you're accused of wanting to keep these areas for an elite few. There are a multitude of places on this planet, or even in British Columbia, that are very beautiful and I'm never going to see them, simply because I don't have the means or the stamina to get there. That is fine with me. As long as I know they are there and that they are untouched, I'm satisfied. I don't have to see everything, or have to feel everything.

The Shape of Time—Carmanah Valley
acrylic watercolor on paper
55 x 37 cm (21³/₄" x 14³/₄")

Audrey Capel Doray

Born in Montreal, Audrey Capel Doray received a B.F.A. from McGill, where she studied under John Lyman, Arthur Lismer, and Gordon Webber. She maintained a painting studio while teaching in Montreal, married in 1956, then studied under William Hayter at Atelier 17 in Paris and at the Central School of Art in London.

Moving to Vancouver in 1957, she taught at the Vancouver School of Art (now the Emily Carr College of Art and Design) from 1959 to 1961. Full-time painting had an auspicious start with a major show at the Vancouver Art Gallery in 1961. She joined the New Design Gallery in 1962. Since then, Capel Doray's work has been exhibited around the world.

By 1967, she had begun to paint on transparent plastic, activating these paintings with lighting and electronics engineered by Bob Mills. These kinetic-audio-light sculptures were featured in ArtsCanada and received critical acclaim across North America.

In the early seventies she moved into experimental film-making. Since then she has returned to paint on canvas, preferring this more abstract means of expressing the shifts and transformations in nature. In the act of painting she comes closer to searching out the essences of changing light, color, edges, and shades.

Capel Doray has received four Canada Council awards. Her work, now represented by the Bau-Xi Gallery in Vancouver, is held in numerous private collections, all major Canadian public galleries, federal and provincial collections, and corporate collections.

This is my second venture into a wilderness area in about a year's time. I went to the Stein Valley last year and loved that experience. To me, as an artist, this is the ultimate work of art and is a nurturing ground for all of us.

I'm very fond of and familiar with trees. I paint in my studio out of my head—not from sketches—but trees, foliage, and sunlight are very much a part of what I do. I always paint with an idea of interlacing light and wind and movement—having things appear non-static. But coming here, the size, the scale, even the moss is unbelievable. I'm trying to create the idea that the trees are like great heavy legs coming down from something very heavenward and to show their relationship to all the other things growing with them.

I'd like this valley to remain exactly as it is. It's very special. We made a mistake a long time ago when we didn't learn how to manage the forest, and, as in every other aspect of life, we've overrun our use of everything. We have to back up and start making corrections and those corrections are going to hurt. If we save this forest, it doesn't mean we cut down another one to make up for it. We simply have to cut back. We certainly shouldn't be taking these wonderful giants and turning them into newspaper.

This is being recognized by people everywhere. It's a global concern. It's interesting that musicians and visual artists are being called in. It's very exciting as an artist to become involved in this, because so often you're painting for a small portion of society. Now I find myself in a milieu that is connected to where we live, which is where art always was in early society. Art was an expression of the life one led and was shared by everyone.

Carmanah Tapestry
acrylic
102 x 76 cm (40" x 30")

Carl Chaplin

Carl Chaplin lives in two very different worlds. In Vancouver, he uses an airbrush and computer to explore leading-edge images, while in the remote northwestern corner of British Columbia he has converted an abandoned power station into a retreat studio where he paints amid the wilderness splendor of the Coast Mountains.

Trained as a biologist, he has an intense interest in the environment and a deep respect for wilderness. Not only does his art advocate a more natural lifestyle, it also warns of the excesses of industrial technology, unrestrained consumerism and nuclear insanity.

He has made the effort to both live that lifestyle and help organize within the environmental and peace movements. His paintings have been helping Greenpeace, UNICEF, and many other groups for twenty years.

Having painted series such as Biospheres, Natural Selection, To Be Continued, *and* Tectonics, *Chaplin and his partner, Linda Bassingthwaighte, are presently organizing a research trip for the series* Ecotopia, *his paintings of Gaia's natural power centres.*

Everyone, except the Brazilian loggers, now agrees that it is imperative that the tropical rainforests be saved. Yet how can we cry "Stop!" while we clear-cut our own forests?

Here in British Columbia, chainsaws work their way closer to the rim of the Carmanah Valley, waiting to make the first cut, while politicians ponder the question of its fate. Sitting in air-conditioned offices, it's easy to be concerned about the loss of hundreds of jobs and millions of dollars. But standing on the forest floor, it is obvious that this is not just a question of a valley full of trees.

The entire ecosystem is interconnected. Trees grow on top of other dead trees. Soil is made of decaying trees from previous generations. Clear-cutting a valley destroys the continuity of regeneration. When the trees are dragged from the forest, the animals leave and rain carries away the topsoil.

The real problem exists on a global scale. We have embarked on a previously untried experiment of cutting down all the trees on the planet, more or less at the same time. Entire regions have been denuded of trees by previous civilizations—and the result has always been disaster. The deserts of the Middle East and Africa are spreading rapidly, where once there were lush forests. It is reasonable to assume that cutting all the world's forests will result in global catastrophe.

The problem is very clear: Earth is in imminent danger. The question of time is now very real. It isn't a job-hungry logger we are trying to stop, but a way of thinking that threatens everything.

This is not the fantasy of an artist's brush, but the predictable math in the wake of our growing numbers. The fate of the Carmanah Valley is just an indicator of our ability to face reality, of whether we are winning or losing the battle to save Earth.

If we seriously believe this is a matter of survival, then we must prevent the first cut.

Chaplin

The First Cut
acrylic on illustration board
76 x 102 cm (30" x 40")

Iris Churcher

Iris Churcher began formal art training in her native England at age sixteen. After five years of study she obtained a B.A. in graphic design from the London College of Printing and embarked upon a career in magazine design. Four years as a designer for the publications Punch *and* Design *left her with the desire for more challenging creative opportunities. This she satisfied by becoming a freelance illustrator and designer and working on projects ranging from book, magazine, and advertising illustration to cushion and toy design.*

In 1978 she immigrated to Canada and continued as an illustrator in Montreal and Vancouver. By 1980 the urge to develop her creativity more fully, coupled with a stay in Santa Fe, New Mexico, caused her to cease commercial illustration. The experience of living close to nature on a small island and on a farm in the Cowichan Valley have also influenced her work. Using mainly the mediums of colored pencil and watercolor, she has explored the art of the mandala and inner vision, the expression of feelings, drawings inspired by nature, and botanical illustration. She currently does commercial illustration and design along with the personal drawings she continues to exhibit.

In the centre of the storm of controversy over whether to log or preserve our forests stand the peaceful Sitka spruce of Carmanah Valley. To walk through this forest is to experience the harmony of plants and animals coexisting, without interference, for hundreds of years. It is living history.

I live in Duncan, where forestry is a big issue and things are becoming polarized. I support the whole move toward preservation. This forest is unique as an environment and doesn't represent a large amount of wood. I am mystified as to why anyone would want to destroy a place that is such a prime example of untouched nature.

This forest is so integrated, blended, and unified. It's a complete, harmonious, peaceful, happy environment—one of the few places left like this. The strongest thing to me is the overall feeling there. I could describe all the foliage—every tiny thing—but the strongest thing I experienced was the total environment, because I was wrapped in it.

Sitting quietly, drawing the root of a giant Sitka spruce, I was surrounded by a sphere of natural sounds. In the distance, the hum of chainsaws pressed in as a reminder of our need to harvest resources for an expanding economy. We live in a very thin layer of the earth's crust and atmosphere. As we turn more and more of this layer into industrial products and polluted air, we have to look closer at those areas that are left untouched. The Carmanah Valley is such an area.

Within the forest time slows. There is time to think, to meditate and reflect upon our relationship to the environment. When we slow down, stress is released, healing takes place, and we are refreshed. Sometimes we forget that we are part of the life cycle of the Earth and that we have a responsibility to keep our home, the planet, clean and healthy. I hope we will preserve many areas like Carmanah as oases of harmony, challenge, and beauty for a society that has much need of their life-giving energies.

Iris Churcher

Unity
colored pencil on watercolor paper
48 x 51 cm (19″ x 20″)

Wesley Clark

Wesley Clark was born in London, England, in 1954. His father's military career brought the family to Canada. A love of nature began with a forested creek bed behind his suburban Oakville, Ontario, home and intensified during adolescent years spent motorcycling and scouting in Alberta's vast prairies. A move to Vernon, British Columbia, introduced him to skiing and canoeing.

Under the guiding influence of teacher and mentor Mike Young, Clark graduated from high school in 1972, excelling in art. Work and travel took him through rugged British Columbia terrain, across Canada, and to Europe, which he toured for five months when he was nineteen. He completed a two-year visual arts diploma at Okanagan College and, at twenty-one, married Elaine. After working and saving (Clark as park ranger, Elaine as hygienist), they embarked on a year-long journey to Japan, the Philippines, Malaysia, Indonesia, Australia, and New Zealand. In 1980, he received a B.F.A. degree from the University of Victoria.

In the past nine years, Clark has developed a respectable understanding of watercolor painting. Influenced by J. W. Turner, Andrew Wyeth, abstract expressionism, and Oriental landscape brush paintings, he relishes combining a loose, active, painterly surface with well-researched subjects. Recent paintings are predominantly of nature, based on his experiences and travels around Vancouver Island. He now resides in Victoria, British Columbia, with his wife and three children.

I came to Carmanah to see the trees and the valley, and to protest the greed of the logging industry. I'm not against logging—I live in a wooden house—but I am against the greed and squandering that's going on. It's pretty obvious that British Columbia is being indiscriminately raped and it has to stop. We have to start listening to all the ecologists and scientists who have been hounding the government for decades now. This whole valley must be preserved to ensure that the ecological integrity of the watershed is maintained.

It's very intimidating inside the forest here; it's such a religious, moving experience. It's important to preserve something like this because in today's world, this is the closest thing we'll ever see to God, to religion, to true beauty. I keep wanting to be naked. It's part of the sensation of being in this primal forest.

Words don't even belong here. What belongs is what's always been here. Total quietude and just the laws of nature.

Carmanah

Don't get sentimental.
Driving dusty, corroded logging
   roads—
like scars on an old whale's back.
See the valleys and mountains—
a sweep of blackened stumps.
See the streams choked with
   discarded timber
and the burning sun frying once-
   shaded ferns.
Proud forests stood here,
Only to fall—to the inevitable.
Clear-cut.
A conglomerate's greed,
   government's endless waste.
Economic crow flies to short-term
   gain.
Why fight the inevitable?

Fall to your knees in awe,
Under the emerald canopy
of Carmanah's gentle giants.
Be moved—inside this ancient
   temple.
Only fragments of our ancient
temperate rainforests remain.
We are the keepers of this planet.
Nothing can replace it,
if it's gone.

Survey Ribbons
watercolor
56 x 76 cm (22" x 30")

Anna-Marie Cobbold

Anna-Marie Cobbold, born in 1951 in Belize, Central America, grew up in Shawnigan Lake on Vancouver Island. She expanded her artistic abilities and political awareness through study in Munich and London, then completed her B.F.A. at the University of Victoria and M.F.A. at Concordia University in Montreal, where she studied with Guido Molinari. With a Canada Council grant, she moved to a Toronto studio in 1981. She served on the board of Mercer Union Gallery, developing new approaches to showing the work of contemporary artists and co-producing a series of New Music concerts. She also designed sets and costumes for Desrosiers Dance Theatre and The Urban Pygmies.

Personal experience and immediate surroundings, always important to her work, were especially pertinent in two 1987 exhibitions. If Only I Had the Heart of a Baboon, *shown after the birth of her son, dealt with the question of abortion. In* Portrait/Facade, *she developed the mediums of charcoal and paint on raw linen and corrugated cardboard.*

The Carmanah experience has coincided with a return to Vancouver Island and marked a synthesis for Cobbold's recurrent theme of man's manipulation of nature. Her work is in corporate collections, the Toronto City Archives, the Canada Council Art Bank, and now has finally found its way home to the West Coast of Canada.

One of the first images to intrigue me was that of a fallen Sitka spruce about 100 metres (330 feet) above the creek (a six-hundred-year distance), its roots still clutching the rocks and gravel of the former creek bed. At first I was confused by these smooth stones embedded in the humus of the forest floor. Not until later did I begin to realize how significant they were as a gauge of time, and how these giant trees had clung onto so very little for hundreds of years. As I walked through the forest I felt a growing reverence for the tenuous aspect of life in this "natural history" museum.

By the third day in Camp Heaven I found that I could no longer stand the searing mental imagery created by the sounds of logging machinery, and I was compelled to revisit the clearcut at the Rosander trailhead. As I came out of the forest, the noise stopped and four men climbed into a crew-cab and drove away. Jobs are important, but logging does not appear to be the noble and collaborative profession it once was. It is an industrialized, mechanized system of destruction, an analogy for much of the world's current economic dilemma. People want to take more and more, with less and less individual exertion and respect, to sell it off for the greatest gain. To what end?

As an artist, I am often faced with creating something out of nothing (or one could say created with that which is God-given). The Carmanah Valley has the spiritual quality of something whole and capable of sustaining itself. This balance of interdependence and self-replenishment can reinforce this same awareness within us. I am grateful that I can continue to draw on this gift since my visit there.

Anna-Marie Cobbold

Shifting Moon River Rocks Clutched by the Roots of the Giant Sitka Dying Regenerating as the River Finds a New Course But for the Tower of Babel
charcoal, acrylic, collage on acid-free corrugated cardboard
152 x 73 cm (60" x 28¾")

Carl Coger

After a Texas childhood of studying Bob Kane and Will James, Carl Coger's advanced art education began with a B.F.A. degree from the prestigious Art Institute of Chicago. He devoted seven years in Europe to travel, study, and commercial art. Five years in the New York City area produced a career in portraiture. Seven years in Oregon created a strong, lasting connection with landscape painting and the West Coast. He immigrated to Canada in 1975, and currently lives in Victoria, British Columbia.

In recent years, all of Coger's nature/landscape paintings have been done in pastel. These may be viewed locally at North Park Gallery and the Art Gallery of Greater Victoria's rental gallery. His portrait work is done in charcoal, pastel, and oil. Coger's oil of Lawrence James Wallace will be installed in October 1989 when renovations of Victoria's Royal Theatre are completed.

Coger's new downtown studio is in Victoria, British Columbia. He is currently active with the Pastel Societies of Canada and America, Island Illustrators Society, and the Fairbank Calligraphy Society.

As an artist and outdoors person, I welcomed this opportunity to combine work and pleasure. My long-term concern about the destruction of our environment dates back to the mid-sixties, when I joined the Sierra Club, began recycling, and informed myself about many of the dangers. Twenty years later, these are again in the headlines, but now with much more urgency.

The excessive greed and waste displayed by current logging practices are only possible in the immoral atmosphere that condones the attitude of "might is right" and "get what you can while the getting's good." Letting big companies have such large tree farm licences is a form of privatization enacted strictly to create a favorable financial ledger, with no concern for the future.

Single voices of protest against this criminal negligence are not as effective as a combined unified front, represented by environmental groups and projects such as this one. Efforts of this sort are necessary to bring awareness to a broader segment of the general public.

Carmanah has become one of the most significantly important areas in British Columbia. I am convinced, not only of the uniqueness and fragility of the valley, but also of how small it is compared to other areas that could be logged. It is rather ironic that my last one-person show focused on a very tiny endangered plant, Macoun's meadowfoam (*Limnanthes macounii*), endemic to southern Vancouver Island, and now I am focusing on our very large endangered old-growth forests.

In the heart of this valley is Dave Parker's Grove, a beautiful spot with a variety of trees of all ages, a few giant spruces, and one dead tree with an enormous base. This huge relic has been mockingly named "Dave" and on it is a plaque which refers to a 1988 newspaper article. British Columbia Forests Minister Dave Parker told the *Vancouver Sun* on June 7 that there are only "three tall trees" worth saving in Carmanah. "They are all but dead, standing on the stump. If you want to preserve them I guess that's fine. . . . A small reserve may be appropriate."

Carl Coger

Twisted Dave
pastel
61 x 43 cm (24" x 17")

Signy Cohen

Born in Winnipeg in 1954, Signy Cohen grew up in a world influenced by the arts, having an architect father and a mother who graduated in fine arts. She moved to British Columbia in 1974 to pursue her own arts education, choosing sculpture at Capilano College in North Vancouver.

A move to the semi-isolation of Maurelle Island, and the creation of three children, renewed her interest in simplicity and spiritual values. The result was beautifully rendered, colored pencil drawings and, eventually, silkscreen prints.

A move to Nanaimo allowed her to further her newfound talents by enroling in Malaspina College printmaking and drawing courses. Her unique creativity now centred in the Nanaimo area, she shares her energy and skills within the arts community. Her endeavors include being a founding member of the Arts 10 Gallery, consulting for and setting up the Nanaimo branch of Imagination Market, and freelance portrait work. To date, she has illustrated three publications with her fine pen and ink work.

She works in the Artist in the Schools program offered by the Madrona Exhibition Centre, and the Arts Alive summer program offered through Nanaimo Parks and Recreation and School District 68, as well as the Parksville and District Youth Arts program. She is also resident artist and a motivating force of the Old School House Gallery and Art Centre in Qualicum Beach.

In Carmanah I felt like a child in a world full of discovery. Along every trail and around every corner, the valley had something new and wonderful to offer.

The enchantment of the valley blew as an ancient wind deep within my soul. The wind was first heard when I came to rest in the quiet of the forest floor. Its sound was that of a great ocean rolling by, high and blue, where the trees met the sky. No wind blew in the depth of the forest; all was still, and then, gently at first, another wind blew. It began deep within my being. I listened to a sound as vast as the universe and looked up toward the giants to see that this sound was within all. I found myself in an ancient cathedral, but even more than this, a living, breathing museum of natural history.

This is a museum to be touched, felt, smelled, experienced. It is a sanctuary, a place for modern man to step out of the fast-paced, high-tech world, to come and be touched within, along its recreational trails, crystal waters, hollow and fallen trees, and many awe-inspiring viewpoints.

Also carried on the wind was the haunting, low howl of the logging equipment as it resumed work after the quiet weekend. It was an uncomfortable sound. On reflection, I realized I had come to this valley to see and experience the spruce groves for myself, as an artist, and to appreciate the beauty, with no intention of taking a political stance. Yet something changed. My heart was won over. The wind I heard this morning was threatening the very being of the trees and life in this valley, a place I had come to love, a gemstone on planet Earth.

Signy Cohen

Forest of Light and Sound
colored pencil on engraved paper
30 x 63 cm (12″ x 25″)

Sue Coleman

Born and educated in England, Sue Coleman gave up her maiden name, Knott, when she married a Canadian and immigrated to Canada in 1967. She quickly fell in love with her chosen country and settled with her husband, Dan, on the southwest coast of Vancouver Island to raise a family.

Having received distinction for her art at Cambridge during her school years, she continued to pursue the arts, trying many different mediums and looking for new and exciting challenges. In 1980, she turned to watercolors, a medium that still delights her today, with new challenges in every painting.

A realist and a romantic, she was completely overwhelmed by the beauty of Vancouver Island and the Pacific Rim. Her paintings often capture those elusive moments when one is at peace with nature, and the pressing crush of modern civilization can be forgotten. She is a supporter of the B.C. Federation of Wildlife, and her awareness of history and culture, and of the delicate balance of the environment and how it can affect the future, is reflected in her work.

There was an intense feeling of peace within the valley. I've felt it before in other locations untouched by man. Every now and then the high-pitched trill of the varied thrush rang through the tree tops, but on the forest floor the sounds were muted, absorbed by huge moss-covered trunks. It was so peaceful I was afraid even to whisper for fear of disturbing the serenity.

Closer to the river there was a breeze and I sat down in the cool shade of a towering clump of trees overhanging the river. I studied the reflections in the still waters running beneath the tangle of roots that formed the bank. Eventually my eyes traveled upwards and I knew I had found the subject matter to portray my feelings for the valley.

I counted fourteen trees growing out of one great root mass, but they were not all the same. There were two Sitka spruce, four alders and eight hemlocks. One hemlock seemed to be growing right out of the trunk of the largest spruce. The roots were tangled around each other, overgrown with such plants as fairybells, false lily-of-the-valley, deer fern, maidenhair fern, false bugbane, foamflower, huckleberry, single delight, and others I couldn't identify, all growing through the carpet of moss.

The spirit of the Carmanah seemed united right here before my eyes. United against the natural forces of the river. United against the elements. United against man.

United We Stand, Divided We Fall

Under a canopy of bird song
That gentle giants hold aloft,
Lies a carpet of mottled shadows
And curtains of hanging moss.

In this house of many seasons,
In this city of the past,
Lies the answer to our future
When the final vote is cast.

In a towering pillar of glass and steel,
The air cooled by great fan blades,
In a room soundproofed from reality,
A decision will be made.

Whether to protect that canopy of
    bird song
The gentle giants hold aloft,
With its carpet of mottled shadows
And curtains of hanging moss.

United We Stand, Divided We Fall
watercolor
56 X 76 cm (22" X 30")

Diana Dean

Diana Dean was born in Africa in 1942. Her first strong memories are of being among the kopjes on the land her family owned near Bulanayo, in what is now Zimbabwe. These huge impelling rocks evoked a sense of wonder. Recently, she learned that certain kopjes were sacred places to the early Bushman and she was convinced that the ones she frequented were such places. This gave her a sense of an existence much greater than her personal life and it is this that has been the driving force behind her work.

In 1952 she discovered a very different world. The silent connection with the large African landscape was replaced with the bustle and fervor of life in England. There, at the age of fourteen, she began to paint seriously on her own, eventually going to the now legendary Bath Academy of Art at Corsham.

Dean's work, apart from the years 1966 through 1976, when she was making sculptures in various mediums, has been predominantly figurative painting. It has been exhibited in England, and since moving to Canada in 1976, mainly at the Nancy Poole Studio in Toronto.

She now lives and works on Saltspring Island, where she teaches art and the violoncello. The landscape here continues to enforce that connection of nature with the spirit of man that she experienced as a young child.

I came to the Carmanah Valley because I wanted to experience the ancient rainforest environment for myself. Now that I am here, I see that it is worthwhile for me to do what I can in order to preserve this special place.

These trees are so extraordinary. They are like huge creatures connected to the earth, their roots like tentacles digging deep down for nutrients. It is as though they are the intermediaries between the Earth and us. Enormous energy comes from them, especially these old trees.

I have always considered trees to be a special part of the world. They are not only visually compelling, but they play a vital part in our ecology. They are the lungs of the living body that is our planet and we need them more than ever now to help maintain the Earth's atmosphere —both now and for the future.

I didn't really know what I was going to do when I arrived, but on the morning of the first day here, I came across the "Big Spruce" and was so overawed by it that I spent most of my time drawing it again and again, trying to get to know it better.

These are magnificent trees that have taken some six hundred years to grow, and we should respect them as part of our national heritage, a priceless birthright.

Diana Dean

Carmanah
oil on canvas
115 X 115 cm (45" X 45")

Michael J. Dennis

Michael Dennis was born in Los Angeles, California, in 1941. He loved animals, bringing home snakes, lizards, octopuses, crayfish, rats, and crows, to the dismay of his mother. Conventionally groomed, he complied obediently with his father's academic aspirations, adopting them as his own.

He studied biology in college (Reed), neurobiology in graduate school (Stanford) and developmental neurobiology as a postdoctoral fellow (Harvard and London). In 1972, he joined the faculty of the University of California medical school in San Francisco. He bought a house, begat a child, and quickly rose from assistant to associate and full professor. What started with a love of animals ended with the decapitation of pregnant rats. Horrified to realize he could spend his life walking the concrete corridors of academe, he quit, immigrated to Canada, and built a home and a life on Denman Island.

In 1984, he went to teach in a medical school in Nicaragua and began to sculpt at the Nicaraguan National Art School. Sculpture soon became the focus of his life. Where logging has decimated our coastal forests, he retrieves limbs of cedar and joins these into figures which often dance. In the woods and sculpting outside, he is with the animals that attracted him in his youth. He is of them—we all are.

The Carmanah Valley is a small paradise, a small piece of what was once all paradise, a rich and wonderful little nook on the edge. It is on the edge of the continent and on the edge of extinction. It is out of the way and relatively inaccessible, which has caused its preservation—until now. Those of us fortunate to visit Carmanah can get a sense of what all of the coastal forests were like before the advent of men with machines. This valley is living history—history of our planet.

The Carmanah Valley represents not only the richness of this Earth on which we live, but also the loss of our understanding and respect for this gift. We are of the land; we share our home with all the other species. We do not own it, though we have come to believe we do. This self-centred view of our relationship to the planet is reflected in the words we use to describe the relationship: ownership, property, resources, development, profit, etc.

We have lost sight of the fact that we are just animals of this Earth. We need to relearn how to live with—as part of—all life. We are now well along in the taking of life from the planet—not only individuals, but entire species. Our own extinction will inevitably follow. The current threat to take life from Carmanah Valley by clear-cut logging is a small example of the blind greed which will kill us. We, the dominating people of this Earth, must change now. We will change, either of our own volition or else by extinction.

Michael Dennis

Hooking for Mr. Greed
cedar slash
76 X 193 X 66 cm   (30" X 76" X 26")

66

Victor Doray

Born in Montreal, Quebec, Victor Doray has lived in Vancouver, British Columbia, since 1957. He received a B.A. from Loyola College in Montreal, and a diploma, Art as Applied to Medicine, from the University of Toronto's faculty of medicine. Though he had previously studied fine arts in New York and Paris, it was during his time at Banff in the fifties that he developed his fascination with the "sky-challenging mountains" of the west. They and the West Coast landscape remain the major inspiration for his paintings.

His paintings are characterized by an expressionistic approach; he interprets the feelings inspired by subjects rather than portraying a strict reality. Watercolors are his preferred medium because they give a mixture of spontaneity, unpredictability, and strength.

He has been working full time as an artist since 1985. Prior to that he was medical illustrator and director of biomedical communications at the University of British Columbia.

Since 1971, Doray has had numerous exhibitions of his work in both public and private galleries and has received a Canada Council senior arts award. His paintings are in collections in Canada and the United States.

Karma-nah

In their presence
you feel humble,
you want to give praise.
It's an exalting experience.
Their sheer grandeur of scale
is beyond human comprehension.
Yet for all their awesome majesty,
they are gentle giants
in a velvet forest called
    Carmanah.
A friendly forest inviting you
to celebrate its soft glory.
Lichens, mosses, and other
    growth,
soften the ground you walk on,
soften colors with soothing
    greens,
soften sounds that are strident
    and near
like chainsaws making bald
    mountains.
Plants retain the rain that
    dampens trails,
even on warm summer days,
    when the sun filters through
diaphanous golden filaments of
    moss
dipping from boughs,
creating well-deserved halos
for these saintly trees.
A sacred place—the oldest, tallest
    Gothic Green Cathedral,
where soaring Sitka columns
crowned by branches
form vaulted archways in the sky.
Exhilarate . . . Breathtake . . .
    Enjoy . . .
Time now to look down the
    purple trunk,
and walk, climb, and touch on an
    endless
journey of fascination around the
    base,
as high roots encircle fallen giants
    and
convolute their way in twists and
    bulges and hollows
among spongy moss and ferns.
To experience a whole forest of
    such ancestral giants
is both a privilege and a
    pilgrimage.
Like Mecca and Chartres, this
    Garden of Eden
must continue to inspire us.

Light Cascade at Carmanah
watercolor on paper
38 X 61 cm (15" X 24")

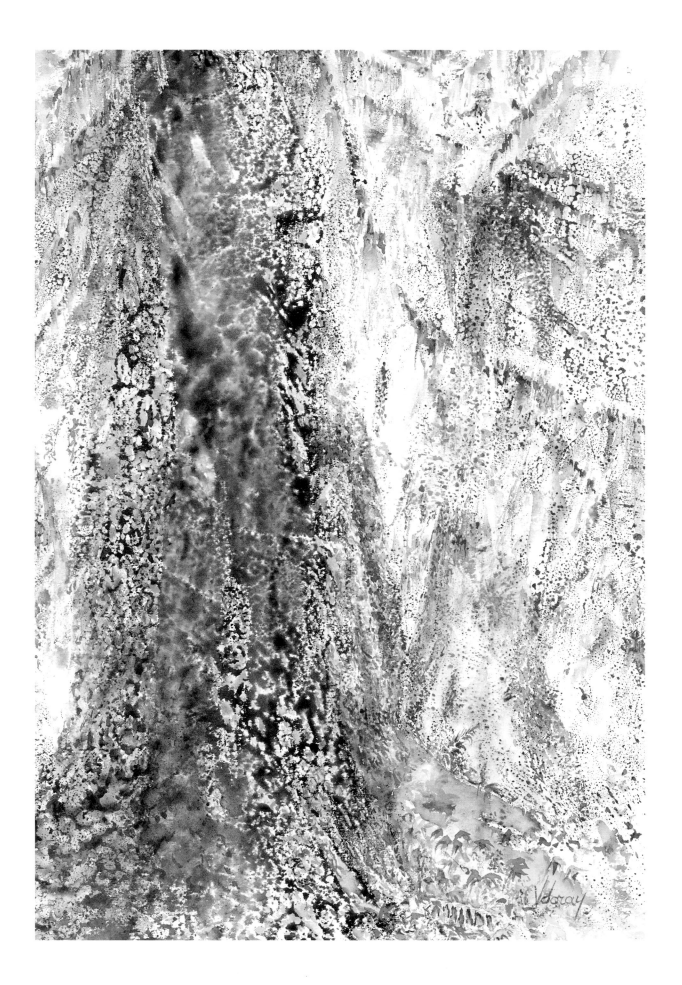

Carol Evans

Born in British Columbia, Carol Evans revels in outdoor living and has painted many areas of the province, including the Queen Charlotte Islands. For the past ten years many of her paintings have been inspired by the almost infinite beauty of the Canadian West Coast.

Her art is expressed through the medium of her exquisitely detailed watercolors. At first glance they seem to have an almost photographic appearance, yet they go far beyond being merely representational.

Evans describes herself as self-taught, although she feels the learning process is never over. Due to hard work and study, plus a rare endowment of natural talent, she has developed an exceptional ability to interpret the essence of her subject, while recognizing the importance of design and composition.

Whether executing a study for a botanical theme, painting a portrait, or rendering a windswept stretch of quiet beach, this artist reveals a thorough mastery of the intricate art of watercolor.

If you spend any time looking at the trees in Carmanah Valley, you start to recognize them as individuals with their own identifiable characteristics. It was this individual quality I wanted to portray, painting them as old people, ancestors. I saw in them the native characteristic of a connection to the Earth. They seemed to be reaching, embracing the sky.

All these individuals, along with the moss, ferns, twittering birds, and other elements of the forest, combine to form a beautifully complete, well-functioning system. There was an abiding sensation of serenity and wholeness during the time we spent moving about within that system.

It is difficult to imagine that a majority of Carmanah is slated for logging. The forest, majestic and silent, stands unprotected in the face of man's voraciousness. While we discuss what to do, the ominous sound of saws filters through the trees as neighboring forests come down.

We have to be protectors now. We have to combine our talents and abilities to save this valley and others all over the world. Our task, as a global civilization, is to work together to heal the Earth and function in cooperation with it. No human soul can be whole or at peace as long as there is the inner knowledge that our Earth is being tortured and slowly dying.

I have every confidence that humankind is capable of restructuring the foundation of civilization to include working in partnership with the Earth. Vast numbers of people around the world are becoming aware of this urgent need for change.

Once, the majority of people believed that the Earth was flat. Now, once again, scientists are reporting their shocking findings and waking up the whole of humanity to face a reality we can no longer ignore.

Between Earth and Sky
watercolor
52 X 71 cm (20½" X 28")

Peggy Frank

Peggy Frank was born in eastern Canada in a small university town. When she was very young, her family moved into a house built by Canadian artist John Hammond. She spent her early, impressionable years surrounded by Hammond's landscapes and seascapes. She became interested in nature, loved to draw and paint, and was intrigued by the ocean.

After earning a degree in marine biology in central Canada, she moved to the West Coast where she has lived for almost fifteen years. Although she has little formal training as an artist, she spent four years drawing wildflowers for British Columbia's Ministry of Forests. Perhaps that is when she began taking her art seriously.

Her love of art and the outdoors drew her toward other artists such as Mark Hobson, Peggy Sowden, and Diana Thompson. They formed an informal partnership and began showing their work in Victoria in 1985, as the Group of Eight. Frank knew they would move on to bigger and better shows, but this group of one hundred artists who care about Carmanah was beyond her wildest imaginings. She is pleased to be part of this group.

I walked into the depth of the forest at Carmanah and wanted to sketch, but I could not. I had to look carefully at the trees, the moss, the ferns, and the flowers; at how the trees broke into the blue sky above; at how they settled into the earth. I had to walk deeper into the forest to forget the horror I had seen the day before. The horror of clear-cut logging, which we cannot allow to continue. "Not here," I whispered. "Please not here." I realized that we, the people of British Columbia, Canadians, had something we had to save, for ourselves and for the rest of the world.

I am a biologist, a resource manager, and an artist. Carmanah is everything that is important to life. It is huge trees stretching up toward the life-giving sun. Carmanah is a carpet of wildflowers, berries, and moss. It is clear water, gravel bars, and mist. It is a place where one finds peace and tranquility, where there is time and space to think and dream. And it is much more, because it is hundreds of years of history and it is tomorrow.

I see Carmanah as a cathedral of the natural world. I wanted to convey the serenity of this place and the sense of awe and wonder I felt in a painting. I found it difficult, because Carmanah was everywhere. It was before me, it was behind me, above and below me. It was here before I knew life and will remain after my life is no longer. Carmanah.

Carnival in Heaven
watercolor
25 x 39 cm (10" x 15½")

Rachel Gourley

Rachel Gourley was born in Yorkshire, England and received her education at the Slade School of Fine Art, University College, London, and King's College, Newcastle-upon-Tyne, where she earned a diploma of education.

Immigrating to Canada in 1966, she became a Canadian citizen in 1969.

She taught art in high school in London and Montreal, then worked as a scientific illustrator in Vancouver and in Oxford.

A friendship with Geneva Jackson and her uncle A.Y. Jackson was influential in the development of her preoccupation with landscape.

She began to use silkscreen as a technique in 1979 and in 1985 she started working at Malaspina Printmaking Society workshop in Vancouver, where she has benefited from the stimulation and friendship of other artists.

It has been a wonderful opportunity to be involved in this project. I have great admiration for what the Western Canada Wilderness Committee has been doing here, and I am grateful to it for providing an extremely interesting and positive experience.

The Carmanah is a most beautiful valley, though presumably no more than most valleys of Vancouver Island once were. It seemed a very special place, with its own magic. The groves of big trees inspired the sort of awe I felt in the great European cathedrals—both have the same grandeur and the same timeless quality.

One day I hiked down the valley toward the ocean—not an easy trail. Following the river, clear and peaceful, the trail climbs up and down and around magnificent trees and lush vegetation. Eccentric-looking ladders scale steep cliffs; slippery, sloping logs span chasms, and ropes appear just when needed. Fallen trees provide welcome relief from mud, tortuous roots, and dense vegetation. The river has made its own way through caverns and rapids. Listening to the musical accompaniment of birds, I felt far away from civilization and in time with the magic of the wilderness.

As the sides of the valley became steeper and the path more a tribute to the ingenuity of the Wilderness Committee trail builders, I noticed a strange hum, like a swarm of bees. It was the ominous sound of a chorus of chainsaws. I stopped beside the river at the Emerald Pool, an enchanting place. The river was gentle here, deep and crystal clear, and astonishingly green.

I shivered as I thought of the desolation that the chainsaws represented. For a moment, I saw this perfect place the day after the logging crews had passed through. It did not seem possible that it could be allowed to happen, but the noise was real. It was not far away!

Rachel Gourley

Emerald Pool, Carmanah Valley
silkscreen
51 x 38 cm (20″ x 15″)

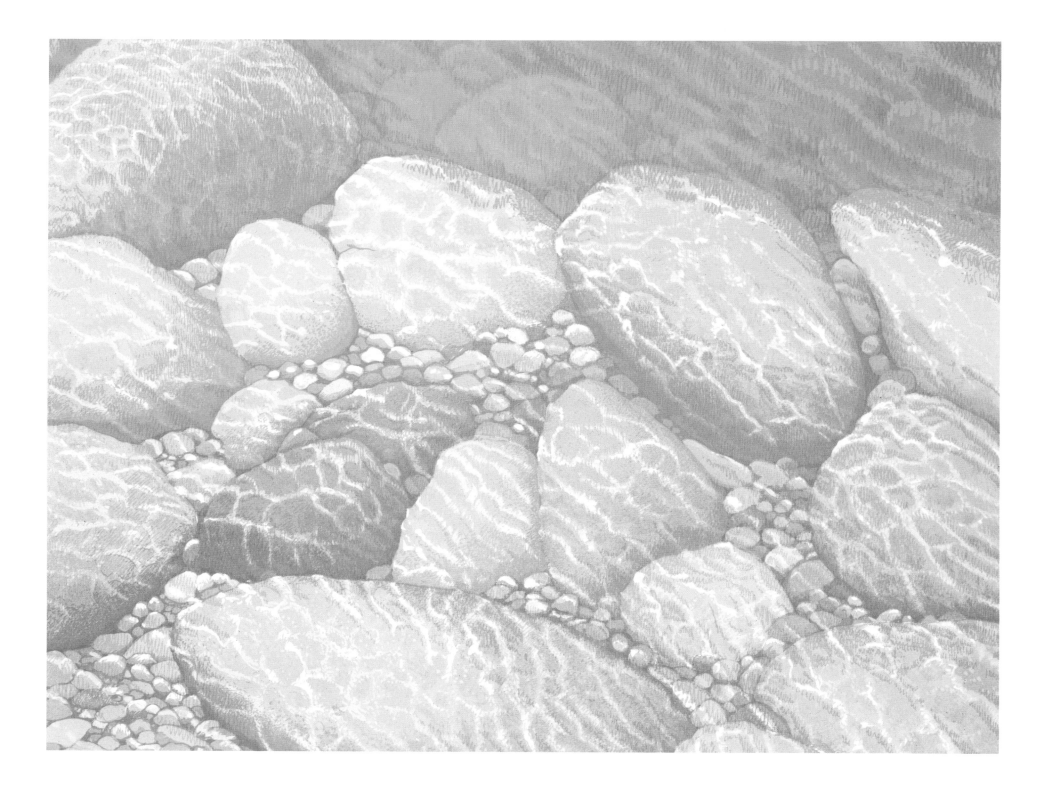

Donald Harvey

Donald Harvey was born in England in 1930 and received his art training at Worthing and Brighton colleges of art. He came to Canada in 1958 and to Victoria, British Columbia, in 1961, where he currently teaches painting and drawing at the University of Victoria.

In the early sixties Harvey established a national reputation as a painter and in 1966 was awarded a Canada Council senior fellowship. He was elected to the Canadian Group of Painters in 1966, the Canadian Society of Painters and Etchers in 1968, and to the Royal Canadian Academy of the Arts in 1970.

Harvey has exhibited widely across Canada, the United States, and Europe. On several occasions, he has represented Canada in selected exhibitions abroad. His work is found in major public collections, including the National Gallery of Canada, the Montreal Museum of Fine Arts, the Charlottetown Confederation Gallery, the Art Gallery of Greater Victoria, the Seattle Art Museum, and the Albright Knox Gallery in Buffalo, New York. The universities of Alberta, Trent, St. John's, Queen's, Scarborough, and Victoria also own examples of his art, as do many corporations such as Toronto Dominion Bank, Imperial Life, Esso Petroleum, Gulf Oil, and CBC.

Donald Harvey is listed in Who's Who in American Art, Canadian Who's Who, *and* International Who's Who in Art and Antiques.

My first really independent paintings, independent of art school tutelage that is, were of greenhouses, gardens and—of all things—golf courses. It is patently clear from these beginnings and my subsequent work that I am centrally interested in organic growth: its freedom and its man-made enforced marriage to structure and geometric order. These concerns are obviously not unique and are as old as painting perhaps. But under whatever guise they reappear in my painting.

The virgin forests of the Carmanah and the Stein did not conform to these personal visual pursuits in painting. Here, in these complex and untouched places, there was no geometry to support me. There were no fences, arbors, grids, or clean straight perspective lines.

This was the challenge of the valleys: to find an order, not imposed by man, but innate in nature.

Each of the wilderness valleys had its own distinct ambience. The Stein, with its ponderosa pines, its openness and pervasive light, was in sharp contrast to the Carmanah, with its lush, labrynthine, overwhelming growth and that wonderful light clawing its way to the forest floor.

These differences meant that I would use different mediums for the two works I have done for the Western Canada Wilderness Committee. Oil pastels and graphite gave me greater conscious control for my work of the Stein, and the very loose process of painting with oil sticks allowed me to become "lost" in the one of the Carmanah.

I can only hope that these two pieces pay appropriate tribute to the splendors of these great wild valleys. I fervently hope that I have met the challenge well and that, in so doing, I and others are successful in the bid to save them for all and forever.

I thank the Western Canada Wilderness Committee for giving me the opportunity to visit the valleys and be party to this project.

The Carmanah Valley
oil stick and graphite on watercolor paper
100 x 74 cm (29" x 39¼")

Linda Haylock

In the four years Linda Haylock has painted professionally, she has participated in two shows with a group of eight nature artists, two solo shows, and various craft fairs.

A third-generation resident, she was raised in the beautiful village of Bamfield, British Columbia. Her childhood years were spent exploring magic rainforests and remote beaches. Boarding away for high school and college, she worked in Victoria and studied massage therapy before returning to work in her family's marine hardware store.

She continues to live in Bamfield, in the house she built with her husband, Cliff, on a small island. Living remotely, amid the spectacular coastal scenery, her subject matter is endlessly inspiring, ranging through wildlife, intertidal life, flowers, scenery, and images of her village home and people. Painting is a solitary pursuit, imparting ongoing personal happiness.

A self-taught watercolor artist, Haylock works mainly from life and specimens. She creates realistic, tightly executed, highly detailed paintings.

Her love of nature goes hand-in-hand with environmental and health concerns. Uneasily aware of global trends toward habitat destruction and the poisoning of our precious earth, she has observed the demise of much-loved forest areas near her home. She is very pleased to be among those participating in preserving Carmanah Valley's unspoiled forest—a legacy for future generations.

To experience Carmanah is to enter a hushed world of giant sword ferns; lavish moss coating logs, branches, and forest floor; enormous, exquisite old trees lit with filtered sunshine. One's entire being is soothed and calmed by the glory of the ancient forest.

The valley is home to many wild creatures, including screech owls. I heard them calling in the evening, which inspired me to paint *Evening Watch*. I wanted to portray a screech owl alert in the tree tops with the last bit of daylight shining behind the spruce in the background.

Such a forest is home to me, having been raised in Bamfield, a small fishing village north of Carmanah. I grew up spending many happy days in similar forests: hiking, collecting mushrooms, identifying wild plants, and watching wild animals.

Being in the forest then and now, marveling at its every aspect, has instilled in me an absolute respect and total appreciation for the treasure we hold in trust. I feel inexpressibly fortunate to have spent time getting to know and love these forests before they were logged. Sadly, many of the forests I knew as a child are now gone, lost to the forest company saws.

We know these old rainforests took thousands of years to develop. Once logged, they will never come back. Knowing this, we can only applaud and support the Western Canada Wilderness Committee and all other organizations and individuals who have the far-sighted wisdom to preserve a few small areas of our glorious rainforest heritage, before it is gone forever.

It is also in the interest of the forest companies to have a few selected areas preserved for their own personal enjoyment, for their families, and for all people now and in times to come. No amount of money can buy back the majesty of an ancient rainforest once it has been destroyed. The Carmanah Valley is one such area, where wildlife and wilderness may flourish among some of our finest old trees, and where future generations may find solace and delight in nature at its finest.

Linda Haylock

Evening Watch, Screech Owl
watercolor on paper
61 x 76 cm (24" x 30")

Graham Herbert

The West Coast is both a home and a source of inspiration for Graham Herbert. His serene and powerful watercolors capture the subtle moods and shifting scenes at the ocean's edge. He is fascinated by the transition from land to sea and sky, and his work investigates the resulting interplay of lines and colors.

He works in a skylit studio atop a hill, surrounded by large trees. There, in a peaceful, rural atmosphere, he distills into paintings the images and impressions that he gathers in his travels along the Pacific coast. Often, the ideas flow into a series of works which revolve around a common theme.

Born in 1947, he studied art at the University of Calgary, the Emily Carr College of Art and Design and the Victoria College of Art. Most of his techniques, however, have resulted from experimentation and innovation. He constantly strives to refine his vision and to intensify his art.

Herbert's work can be found in many private collections and in major galleries in Canada and the United States. He has had several one-man shows and participated in many group exhibits. Television interviewers and journalists have presented programs and articles about him, his art, and his lifestyle. A constantly expanding following is finding pleasure in the unique and special qualities of his work.

Time. Carmanah speaks softly about the gentle rhythms of passing time. For centuries the creek has meandered back and forth across the valley floor, where spruce establish themselves and send shallow roots creeping across the gravel. The massive trees are held in a delicate balance, like indigenous totems whose spirits fill the valley. Nature's rhythm is slow and regenerating.

A valley like Carmanah is a place to pause and reassess our actions; it is an opportunity to soak up nature's ways and to share the generous perspective presented by an ancient forest. As the population grows and our demands escalate, we threaten to imprison ourselves in a world of noise and haste—ever more people and diminishing wilderness.

My hope is that, through painting this magnificent valley, I will communicate the importance of saving a delicate ecosystem that has taken centuries to create. A few days wandering among the giants, letting their pulse replace my own, have given me a rare tranquility. I attempt to capture this emotion in my watercolors, but it isn't easy. The feeling is elusive, more easily experienced than depicted.

In Carmanah the sounds I hear are music: bird songs, wind sighing in the trees, and the creek singing over the stones. Monday, 8 a.m., man-made sounds invade—the roar of diesel engines from heavy logging equipment outside the valley. It reminds me that they want to devour Carmanah and leave behind a token strip of spruce. People will be able to drive in and see the big trees, isolated in a doomed environment and surrounded by clear-cut hills. They won't be able to ease slowly into the mood of Carmanah and feel the rhythm of the forest. No deep and renewing thoughts are likely to come from a paved parking lot.

I have been fortunate to visit Carmanah before the insatiable demon has been let loose to scratch and claw the hillsides. Nurtured by the ancient trees and soothed by the creek, I have been inspired to paint my feelings for the valley, in the hope that Carmanah will remain unviolated for its own innate qualities.

GRAHAM HERBERT

Calm Waters Whispering
watercolor
75 x 56 cm (29½" x 22")

GRAHAM HERBERT

Mark Hobson

Mark Hobson has been painting scenes of British Columbia's west coast since he first visited Long Beach as a teenager. The route to becoming a full-time artist, however, has not been particularly direct. As a child he drew animals and the natural world almost daily, subsequently teaching himself skills in the use of watercolors and acrylics. Later, as he followed a path toward a biology degree, the opportunity to devote time to art faded and was almost shelved during the nine years he taught sciences at Shawnigan Lake School near Duncan, British Columbia.

Ideas for canvases kept smoldering in the background, however, and in 1983 he decided to break from teaching to make more time for painting. A seasonal job as a park interpreter directing the Wickaninnish Centre at Pacific Rim National Park left the winter months free for creativity and was the perfect transition toward painting full time. Mark now makes his home in Tofino on Vancouver Island, surrounded by the rugged beauty and drama of the outer coast so frequently depicted in his work.

The outer fringe of British Columbia's coast holds a special fascination for me. As a photographer and painter, a recurring theme in my work is the coast forests. The infinite array of shapes created by gnarled trunks and moss-laden branches inspires endless challenges. Yet in the last few years a far greater challenge has become the urgent need to prevent the destruction of the very things that attracted me to the West Coast in the first place.

A recent satellite photo tells the story blatantly. Except for three patches along the western edge, representing the Brooks Peninsula, Clayoquot Sound, and the Carmanah Valley, Vancouver Island has lost all significant examples of its original rainforests. To have these last refuges join the endless hectares of clear-cut slopes and monotonous rows of replanted seedlings would be as criminal as dismantling the pyramids to build apartments.

The value of the experience evoked by walking in a thousand-year-old forest such as the Carmanah Valley is impossible to equate in dollars and cents. There is an immense wealth in the ferns and randomly scattered decaying logs, but like a sky darkened with passenger pigeons, we can only assess such riches once we have lost them forever. Within the next ten or twelve years, if cutting continues at its present rate, Vancouver Island's old-growth forests will be reduced to memories. As residents of British Columbia, it is our entrusted responsibility to the rest of the world to ensure that this does not happen.

A mixture of old growth and the more open terrain caused by logging creates good habitat for deer and elk. The intense cutting in recent years, however, has removed a large number of the patches of old growth, vital for winter survival. The Roosevelt elk in this painting are confused and alert, as their once-familiar routes through the forest are being drastically altered by clear-cutting and a slash fire. Smoke from the fire, despite its ominous presence, provides a perfect backdrop to enhance the grandeur of the forest.

Mark Hobson

Refugees
acrylic
76 x 97 cm (30" x 38")

Dorset Huntingford

Born in British Columbia in 1952, Dorset Huntingford was raised on the West Vancouver waterfront, one of a family of five children. She has always had a strong connection with nature due to family sailing weekends, beginning at age three. As a child she "lived" nature, scrambling along the shoreline, sailing, and bushwhacking along the British Columbia coast. Nature has always commanded her respect and been a source of inner strength. Consequently, it is an integral part of her work.

Her interest in art began at an early age. She was constantly drawing animals, boats, trees, and people. Her father, a naval architect, was her first real inspiration, drawing wonderful Spanish galleons at her request.

A serious interest in art deepened upon enrolment at the Vancouver School of Art (now the Emily Carr College of Art and Design). Working mainly in oils at the time, she changed from a traditionally realistic style to large-scale abstraction and color-field, non-subjective works. After that enjoyable, intense period came the reality of paying off student loans, and she worked for a large corporation for a number of years.

There was, however, always a desire to get back to full-time art, not just sporadic painting, drawing, and photography. Once she made that decision, Huntingford's life and artwork have strengthened each other, until now there is no separation between them.

Carmanah Valley and all her splendor has played a very large part in my life since my first visit in October, 1988. I call Carmanah "she" as one uses the term to describe the gender of a boat, which also has a gift of freedom and life.

As we drove from Victoria to Carmanah, accompanied by family and friends, we certainly noticed the clearcuts enroute. We resigned ourselves to the fact that logging is mostly done this way in British Columbia and, of course, we had seen it all before. However, after spending eight hours hiking in Carmanah, overwhelmed with all its mystery and haunting beauty, we were no longer resigned. I have been angered and remain so at the loss of some of my favorite special spots to logging—places such as Hardy Island (up the coast) and an old-growth forest with a salmon stream at the head of Long Bay on Gambier Island.

My husband, Derek Young, and I knew we could not rest with the thought of Carmanah also meeting such a fate. He immediately contacted the office of the Western Canada Wilderness Committee in Vancouver and we obtained our road guide to the valley. After many months of organizing and gathering support in Victoria, Derek has opened the first official branch there and has become one of the directors of the Wilderness Committee.

My own contribution to Carmanah, besides my work with the Wilderness Committee, is to hope you can feel, through my art, at least a touch of the magic, timelessness, and sheer joy of life that exists in the one and only Carmanah Valley. It is my desire to pull your heartstrings, so that you can feel the pulse of her. May Carmanah remain forever untouched, a legacy of how we, the people of the world, had the clarity and insight to preserve this enchantment.

Cradled in Carmanah
watercolor
59 x 76 cm (23" x 30")

LeRoy Jensen

LeRoy Jensen was born in Canada in 1927 and brought up in China and Japan. He received his art training at the Academy of Fine Arts in Copenhagen, Denmark, and in Paris with André L'Hôte. He returned to Canada in 1954, where he taught painting with the Extension Department of the University of British Columbia, at the Banff School of Fine Arts, and in the Okanagan.

Jensen's work has been exhibited extensively throughout Canada and the United States in both solo and group shows. His work can be found in the collections of the National Gallery of Canada and the Burnaby Art Gallery.

I deeply appreciate the privilege of entering this place and being surrounded and enfolded by this great power in nature. It will be perpetual, as long as it is left to grow and develop as it should.

This delicate, yet immensely powerful, stability in nature reflects the reality of mankind—we are rooted in the earth, and develop according to particular laws of which we are almost totally ignorant.

What a crime it would be to jeopardize this creation. I do not understand it, but I may, through respect, come in closer contact with both myself and the forest.

Painting is movement, luminosity, and a discovery of the rhythm that underlies a subject. I must find the proper blend of these forces and set them free; then the reality appears by itself.

Having done numerous works on the theme of the Carmanah, I chose this, which represents the genesis of the forest. It suggests the bottom litter, the growth of a tree, and the suggestion of the restless river winding through, shown in the flashes of white.

Being in contact with this wonderful natural display has made clear to me how little we humans know of what surrounds us or of what we are. We hear so-called experts telling us what to think and what to do with both nature and ourselves, but I am unable to believe their glib pronouncements.

First there is nature and life; then money and jobs. If there was more concern for the former, the latter would have less influence, and natural dignity would be preserved.

Genesis
pastel
76 x 115 cm (30" x 45")

Nola Johnston

Born in Edmonton, Alberta, in 1954, Nola Johnston lived for five years as a child in Yellowknife, Northwest Territories. This left an abiding love for the North and a determination to get back there as often as possible. Since the age of nine she has lived in the Lower Mainland of British Columbia.

In 1977, she graduated from the Vancouver School of Art (now Emily Carr College of Art and Design) with an advanced diploma in graphic design. Since then she has worked in this field, primarily as a freelancer, concentrating in later years mainly on illustration. Major projects have included producing illustrations for native language education programs with several bands in British Columbia and Washington state, particularly a one-year project with the Kwagulth in Alert Bay. She has also done extensive natural history interpretive work for clients such as the British Columbia Ministry of Parks.

In the last six years she has turned from a couch potato into a born-again outdoor recreation enthusiast, with a particular passion for whitewater canoeing. So far she has been unable to find anyone who will pay her to indulge herself by spending time in the wilderness.

I would like to see the Carmanah Valley saved in its entirety; for many reasons it's extremely important to keep places like this. It's very impressive. I've been overwhelmed by the trees, the size of them, the proliferation of nature. It just kind of struts and foams in every direction.

In the long term, logging a place like this is shortsighted. There are other alternatives and solutions that can support the needs of forestry and the economy without destroying such a valuable treasure. What is needed is the energy and will to look for them.

I'm trained as a graphic designer and graphic designers are taught that the primary function of their art is communication. This applies to all forms of art; the most effective is that which communicates the best. Artists interpret the world around them and beyond that, they interpret their social reality. You reflect through the lens of your own vision what you see, but it will be translated in terms of your particular culture, in effect contributing to the creation of a social mythology.

Our Western civilization has generally considered nature to be something very separate and dangerous —an enemy to be controlled and conquered rather than something we are a part of. This is reflected in the attitude of many people toward wilderness. On the other hand, the approach of traditional native Indian cultures shows a much greater sense of harmony with the natural world. Our society, if it is going to survive, needs to move toward that kind of social mythology of unity—a recognition that we're all part of the same living organism.

Artists can try to reflect and create this new kind of social vision in terms of the wilderness and our connection with it. That's how I see projects like this—where artists come into places like Carmanah —fitting in: trying to construct a new way of looking at things.

Winter Wren
oil on canvas
46 x 61 cm (18″ x 24″)

Bege Johnston

Born in Victoria, British Columbia, in 1948, Bege Johnston has lived on islands all his life, from Saltspring to the Queen Charlottes.

Having no formal art training, he has been entirely influenced by the environment that is so much a part of his natural talents. The magic of the West Coast rainforest and the ever-changing life-force of the ocean have inspired this artist in his chosen medium of native and exotic woods.

Spiritual inspiration, West Coast culture, and a boundless imagination allow him to create images within a wide spectrum of styles and concepts. His works vary from deep mystical reflections and sensual expression to a rather unorthodox sense of humor.

Johnston is presently producing carvings and drawings and is a resident artist and founding member of The Old School House Gallery and Art Centre in Qualicum Beach, Vancouver Island, British Columbia.

Birth, growth, life, death, re-birth! The Carmanah rain forest is thousands of years of unhindered evolution; an interdependence unparalleled in the world; a magic that once was all of the British Columbia coast lands.

Soft black mud greets each footfall along the meandering path through fern and skunk cabbage, the pungent odor permeating the still air. Entwined fingers of twisted, gnarled roots appear through the sparse underbrush, forming a subterranean wooden puzzle beneath the forest floor. Massive cedars stand vigil over the entrance to the valley below, the trail switching back and forth into a world so breathtaking, so captivating, that time is no longer the controller and fantasy is indeed the reality. The light is filtered green through a distant ceiling of spruce and fir; only here and there are shards of sunlight allowed to pass.

The fallen giants have become nourishment for rows of seedlings, which will be the forest of the next generation.

Only at the creek bed is the foliage sliced to open sky. Here salal grows beyond a man's reach and the magic of the giant Sitka spruce begins with the seemingly insignificant sprouting of a single seed.

The Carmanah watershed shelters and nurtures giant Sitka spruce, fir, hemlock, alder, and ancient cedars. Cradled by steep valley walls, this forest is host to myriads of species which comprise the lush vegetation and provide natural habitat for abundant wildlife. This valley asks nothing of the self-appointed managers of this planet but simply to exist!

To exchange such a unique, stable environment for something as unstable as a dollar bill, destroying forever one of the remaining first-growth forests on Vancouver Island, is not only criminal but insane!

Could the saving of this extraordinary ecosystem for perpetuity be, instead, an opportunity for human beings to share in intelligent evolution for the benefit of all, rather than the momentary gain of a few? I, for one, sincerely hope so.

Bege Johnston

Winds of Carmanah
western redcedar intended for chipper mill
33 x 53 x 25 cm (13" x 21" x 10")

Erika Kertesz-Green

Erika Kertesz-Green is a full-time artist and designer living in Vancouver, British Columbia. She has been drawing and painting since childhood. Among her favorite subjects are nature, exotic flowers, and antique dolls. She tries to convey her feelings, using the medium of watercolor to portray form, color, and depth.

Kertesz-Green finished art school in Hungary. Since arriving in Canada, she has attended art classes at the University of British Columbia and has studied with master watercolorist Zoltan Szabo in Hawaii and Oregon.

Her works are in corporate and private collections here in Canada, as well as in the United States, Australia, and Europe.

I have always loved nature. The happiest moments of my life are connected with it. I feel at ease and at home between mountains, in forests, and in meadows. Nature inspires, soothes, and excites me at the same time. That's why my experience in the Carmanah Valley was one of the highlights of my adult life. The thousand-year-old trees awed me, and the spiritual bond with fellow artists made me feel hopeful that there is still time to stop or turn back the destruction.

Coming from the small country of Hungary, I felt lost among the huge giants. My attention focused on the beautiful variety of life carving out an existence in the shadows of the forest floor. Nature is wonderful. There is room for all creatures to be hidden, protected, and nurtured by each other in the universe of the rainforest.

If only I could forget the devastation I saw on the perimeter of the valley enroute to Carmanah! My heart sank at the sight of mammoth machinery gobbling up the forest, creating devastation with every step.

It is hard to believe that decent people with clear consciences would want to change this beautiful rainforest into a terrible rubble heap —for money! If it took thousands of years for the trees to grow, what hope have our children—the future generation—to see rainforests like Carmanah. We must take measures to save it now.

To fight for our inheritance and natural treasures is everyone's responsibility, and it makes me feel happy and proud to be part of this effort through my art.

Erika Kertesz Green

Valley Twins
watercolor
46 x 51 cm (18" x 20")

Lynda Laushway

Lynda Laushway was born in Peterborough, Ontario, in 1950. Raised in the Ottawa Valley, she studied fine art at the University of Guelph and then proceeded to complete a masters degree in applied criminology at the University of Ottawa. She has been a practising professional visual artist for the past eleven years, specializing in printmaking. After working at St. Michael's Printshop in Newfoundland for six years, she moved to the West Coast in 1984. She now lives on Saltspring Island and travels to Vancouver to do her artwork at Malaspina Printshop on Granville Island.

Laushway's etchings have been exhibited throughout Canada and in other parts of the world. Her work can frequently be seen in both solo and group exhibits in the Vancouver and Victoria/Gulf Islands areas. Work from her most recently completed exhibition, entitled Rape of Gaia, *was part of a group show in Peru and and traveled to Finland and Scotland.*

I feel a strong commitment to try to do what I can to preserve our environment—not only for our generation, but for future generations to come, so that they can experience the beauty and wonder of nature as well.

Carmanah is a sacred place. There's no question in my mind about that. I am humbled by the power, beauty, and incredible dignity in these old trees. I feel very privileged to be here.

It is the power, grace, and dignity of the forest that I would like to be able to record. As an artist I feel frustrated in trying to capture the wonder of these trees. I would like to be able to give people who see my work a sense of what it was like to be here.

There is no question in my mind that this whole valley has to be saved. This is a national treasure, if not a world-class treasure. It must be saved so that fifty years from now, people will be able to come and have this same very privileged experience. We owe this to our children.

Part of my feeling of frustration and sometimes even anger is the lack of respect I see the powerful segments of our society showing toward nature. We've moved so far away from respecting and honoring the wonderful gift that we have around us in the form of natural beauty. We have to return to that respect if we want to survive on this planet. We must start giving something back, not just taking all the time.

Lynda Laushway

Carmanah Lights
etching
45 x 61 cm (17³/₄″ x 24″)

Don Li-Leger

The work of Don Li-Leger reflects his lifelong love of nature. Born in British Columbia, he has painted since childhood. Initially focusing on the wildlife native to his province, recently he has been exploring the wealth of inspiration to be found in sanctuaries throughout North America and abroad.

Li-Leger has studied at the Vancouver School of Art (now the Emily Carr College of Art and Design), the Banff Centre School of Fine Arts, and Simon Fraser University. His paintings have been exhibited throughout North America, including the prestigious Leigh Yawkey Woodson traveling exhibit, as well as being represented in numerous private collections.

Li-Leger makes his home at Crescent Beach, British Columbia, along with his wife Cora, also an artist, and their two children.

It is a humbling experience to be among such ancient spruce. Standing beneath these immense trees, gazing skyward along trunks more than three metres (ten feet) in diameter, one feels truly small and insignificant.

Looking through the grove at daybreak, the spruce form an awesome silhouette. As the sun captures the mountain, it casts blue shadows which, with the smattering of yellowish green alders between, provide the perfect backdrop to the huge moss-laden spruce trees.

The picturesque valley is an idyllic palette of ever-changing color and contrast. As I sat on a cool gravel bar near Carmanah Creek, I was delighted to find a brilliant display of western columbine and further surprised to hear the familiar hum of a male rufous hummingbird, as he came to feed among the flowers. Rich and ripe with life, this is but one of the priceless natural vignettes which collectively represent the magic that is the Carmanah Valley.

I would like to see the entire valley preserved for this and future generations. This is a pristine environment—the water is crystal-clear and clean to the taste, and there is almost no sign of human presence.

We in British Columbia are privileged to have such wilderness areas within our borders; we should take the global responsibility to make environmental conservation of paramount importance.

Along Carmanah Creek
acrylic
27 x 42 cm (10¾" x 16½")

Peter Lynde

Peter Lynde is one of many painters who have enriched the field of gallery art from a background in the commercial art industry.

Born in London, England, in 1946, he arrived on Vancouver Island in 1948. Upon graduation from high school, he left Nanaimo to attend the Vancouver School of Art (now the Emily Carr College of Art and Design), and subsequently, the Alberta College of Art in Calgary.

In 1970 he began work as a commercial designer and illustrator, and two years later he set out as a freelance illustrator. His work was soon in demand by major advertising agencies in Vancouver, Calgary, and Edmonton, and over the next sixteen years he took part in many award-winning projects.

Teaching in the Vancouver school board adult education program and conducting seminars for commercial art students at Capilano College have allowed him to share his experience. More recently, he has given painting demonstrations in Vancouver area schools as well as to adult painting groups.

Lynde has been painting full time since October, 1988. He has won awards at Federation of Canadian Artist exhibitions and been selected for the 1989 San Diego Watercolor Society international exhibit. In February 1989, he was elected associate of the Federation of Canadian Artists.

He makes Saltspring Island his home and is represented by Pegasus Gallery in Ganges, and Gulf of Georgia Galleries in Steveston.

My first visit to the Carmanah Valley was for five golden spring days. As I began the descent into the valley, my senses were warmed by the sights and sounds that accompanied the swinging of a remarkably heavy pack; the sunny smell of cedar and fir, scattered bird song in a cool blanket of silence, bootprints in the moist earth, the friendly handiwork of trail-builders. My sense of awe grew as I was swallowed by vast emerald curtains of rainforest.

As my feet explored the valley floor, I gradually recognized that I was in very special company: trees incomprehensibly ancient and massive that soothe with a voice irresistibly powerful, that gently urge the imagination to understand.

How to understand when bird song is accompanied by the moans of nearby logging machinery, waist-deep in the ghastly remains of a forest's shattered foundations?

The mountainsides are covered with timber declared too valuable to be left standing, slated for clear-cutting.

My senses, between the caress of green velvet and the rattle of hot steel, collapsed into anger. My anger was not directed at the loggers. The men cutting trees up there, workers in an industry that is part of British Columbia's heritage, are victims as much as I am of a system whose weakness is all too human. Instead, I wished the companies' shareholders and directors and the government officials could be standing with their families on this valley floor, for it is their demands that determine the course of the forest harvest.

I wept—a helpless, angry victim surrounded by a so-called renewable resource that is not being renewed. Around me, the forest seemed unconcerned. The spruce giants towered, massive, silent, dignified; the delicate ferns swayed gently in pools of sunlight; the birds sang from invisible depths.

I gradually heeded the forest's gentle urging to take up my little box of pencils and paints and offer my small part, adding my voice to the desperate cry for a new appreciation of Earth's fragile treasures whose abundance seems matched only by humanity's most cruel vice: greed.

Spirit Dialogue
watercolor on paper
54 x 73 cm (21" x 29")

Patrick Mahon

Thirty-two rings have formed within the giants of Carmanah since Patrick Mahon was born, and while most of that was happening, he was many hundreds of miles distant. Born in Winnipeg, Manitoba, he spent all but the past three years of life there, living and working. He received a B.F.A. and an education certificate from the University of Manitoba. He subsequently taught native students in Winnipeg's inner city for five years, becoming educated to a variety of concerns in that vital community. The next two years, 1986 and 1987, were spent alongside his spouse teaching in Chesterfield Inlet, Northwest Territories, a tiny Inuit community. During his seven years as a school teacher, Mahon continued drawing and printmaking, often as a means of expressing what he perceived through teaching aboriginal students.

The Mahons moved to Vancouver from the North in June, 1988, and Patrick has worked as a printmaker at Malaspina Printmakers on Granville Island since then. He teaches part-time, and is preparing to do his M.F.A. at the University of British Columbia. Coming to the West Coast has provided an opportunity to enlarge his awareness of environmental issues and to relate them to the concerns of the native Indian and Inuit people whose children he has taught.

During my stay at Carmanah, I wondered how to produce something of beauty in a place where the setting itself seemed bent on "upstaging" anything I might try to do. Using charcoal from an old campfire and red pigment from decaying cedar, I drew on a fallen, dried log. I intended it to be a temporary piece that would not permanently intrude on the environment; I photographed it and washed it away. To my surprise, a faint ghost remained, reminding me of the virtual impossibility of leaving the environment we cherish untouched by our presence.

Looking out now from my Kitsilano suite, I view a vast stand of dwellings, extending layer on layer, farther than I can see. I try to imagine a forest as crowded; groves of spruce and fir as persistent as those condominiums.

To remember Carmanah, I have to look through the tunnel of unfolding summer days, over a logging road that choked us with dust, and down a rocky, shadow-strewn trail to find the forest. Then I must remember the hours between cups of tea and conversations, between the speculations about the "facilities," reminding us of our frailty in those places.

I'm from the prairies, where forests are rare exceptions in the landscape. For me, trees have always been associated with a sense of relief from the unbroken horizon line and unyielding summer sun. The feeling of relief in the Carmanah forest is palpable.

To be in Carmanah is to be embraced both physically, by the great, softly rounded columns which surround, and spiritually, by the deeply rooted and interconnected system of nature that celebrates the interdependent life of our world. To be there is to be dwarfed by the magnitude of the trees and to feel the grandeur of space. Most especially it is to be aware and unaware of time, and to know that our hours in the forest are but a few of the millions of hours that have passed, and must pass, in the presence of those trees.

Patrick Mahon

Carmanah Apology
woodcut-collagraph on paper;
Cibachrome of a drawing on a log,
in charcoal and cedar pigment
75 x 55 cm (29 1/2" x 21 3/4")

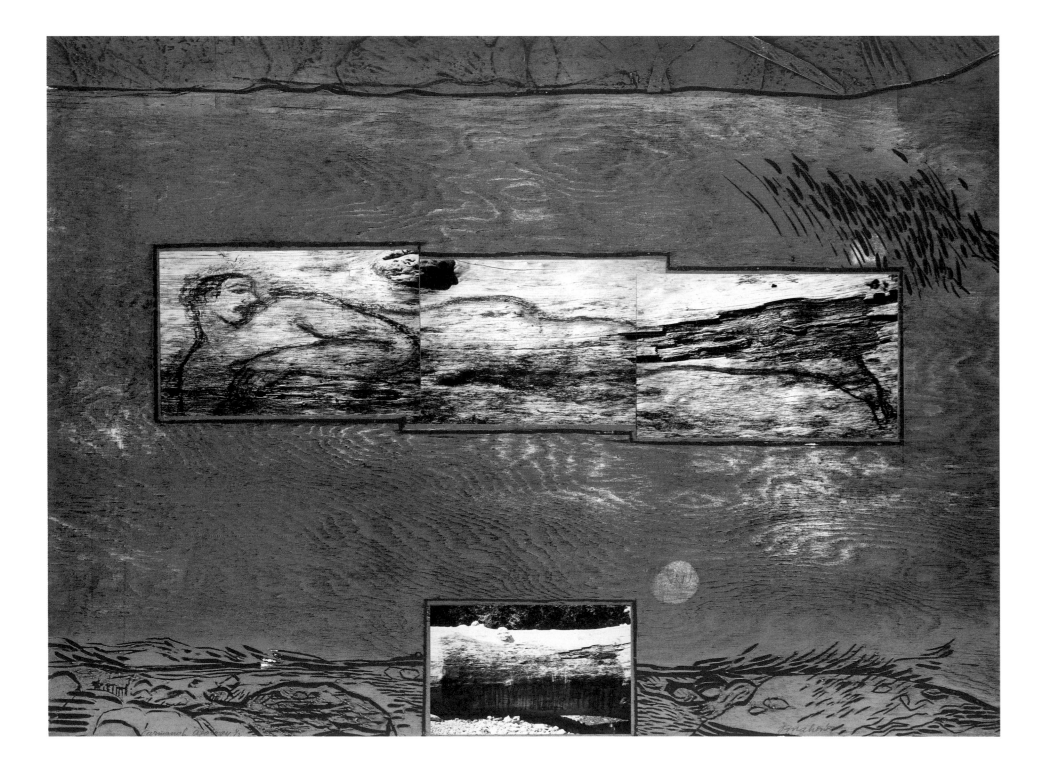

Gretchen C. Markle

Gretchen Markle came late to art as a vocation. Growing up in northern Ontario, she was constantly doodling, but had little opportunity to expand her artistic horizons. Art wasn't even on the school curriculum. Science was, however, and her love of nature led her to obtain an honors B.Sc. in biology and do graduate work in forestry at the University of Toronto.

She continued to draw, but it was a sporadic hobby for pleasure. It was to her surprise, then, that when she applied to the British Columbia Provincial Museum as a marine biologist, they hired her to illustrate their natural history exhibits, handbooks, and education projects. It was repetitive work, so after a few years, she left to do other things. Art once again took a back seat to her primary occupations, but the seed had been sown. Two years ago, the need to be visually creative won out, and she quit her teaching job to take up art full time.

Since then, Markle has been exploring the possibilities of dyes on silk. Using a method that is almost a cross between batik and wet-on-wet watercolor, she applies liquid dyes to silk to produce both frameable paintings and wearable art. While she often depicts natural subjects in these paintings, she eschews illustration in favor of vibrant color and semi-abstract form.

Visiting the Carmanah Valley has been a very profound experience for me. I have spent much of my life in forests, but that doesn't take anything away from the wonder and awe I feel here. It isn't merely the size of the trees, it's the serenity of this valley that is so transcendent.

This tranquility must surely arise from the wholeness of the valley. It has never been ravaged by unnatural forces. Rather it has evolved on its own into the complex, stable ecosystem that it is today.

What gives man the right to endanger such a treasure? We wouldn't dream of tearing down the apse of Chartres Cathedral as a make-work project. It would be folly to destroy one of the world's great architectural and religious masterpieces for dubious short-term gain. Similarly, we can't log part of the Carmanah Valley without destroying the integrity of one of nature's great physical and spiritual masterpieces. We should recognize that some places have an inherent right to exist, just as they are. They should be kept for their own sakes, and damn the cost.

I debated about how to convey my feelings for the Carmanah in a simple piece of art. In the end, I decided to celebrate its loveliness rather than depict the shocking contrast of lush valley to desolate clearcut. I felt that if I managed to even hint at its beauty, perhaps more of the general public would make the effort to visit the Carmanah and fall under the spell of its harmony.

As a subject, I chose Carmanah Creek itself, since it epitomizes the entire valley. Survival of its pristine clarity depends directly upon the unlogged integrity of the ecosystem.

Gretchen Markle

Carmanah Kimono
dyes on silk
(Couturier: Tricia Cadorette)

Morgan McKay

At age seventeen, Morgan McKay left behind a conservative Oak Bay upbringing to live on the West Coast of Vancouver Island. Here she began to explore the extraordinary forest and ocean landscape, working with paint, as well as whalebones, sticks, stones, earth, and feathers. Introduced to native culture, she was influenced by artists Joe David, Godfrey Stephens, and Roy Vickers.

In the fall of 1979, she moved to Vancouver to study fine art at the Emily Carr College of Art and Design. Then, back in Tofino, she designed fund-raising graphics for the Save Meares Island campaign. Her artistic activism also led her to erect political signs along the highway to Tofino.

With Meares Island spared from MacMillan Bloedel's chainsaws, McKay returned to Victoria for further studies in fine art, and spent two seasons tree-planting. In the fall of 1987, she moved to Saltspring Island and began constructing her first native shield of sticks, feathers, and stones.

Long fascinated by Navaho sand paintings, ancient petroglyphs, and the use of the circle to invoke the integrated wholeness of all life, she found it only natural to create a series of mandalas the following winter. Further explorations in a life that has become mandalic include a sign on Saltspring facing the Crofton pulp mill and earthworks high on Mount Maxwell.

The descent into Carmanah Valley feels like entry into a womb-like place of the earth. Ordinary life fades away, and we are filled by the deep, mysterious wonders of our world. Out of silence and solitude a wisdom, probably much greater than ours, can be sensed among these ancient giants. It stirs, deep within, some memory of our origins and our primal ties with the ebb and flow of the universe.

In Carmanah, I slept upon a green mossy bed, curled up beside a giant spruce, and woke to the sound of grapple yarders working nearby. My dreams were shattered. The sanctity of Carmanah has already been violated, but the spirit of Carmanah roars with a thunderous silent message, far beyond the power of industry.

Having been a tree-planter, I have seen the horror of clear-cut logging and countless, failed attempts at re-forestation. If only all people could see behind the facades of "Forests Forever," "Super Natural B.C.," and the narrow strips of forest along many provincial highways, and realize that most of what is left is slated for clear-cutting in the near future. The replanted forests will not continue to support the rich and varied forms of life they once did. They are timber farms: trees planted in rows; only one or two species in vast areas; and loaded with captan, 2, 4-D, and other chemicals.

Industry would like to keep us busy squabbling over jobs while it continues clear-cutting, accelerates production, and increases profits. At current rates, the entire Carmanah watershed could be clear-cut in eight days!

Preserving the whole Carmanah Valley and other places like it around the globe has become a matter of human survival. Industry must join us in our evolution toward reintegrating ourselves and our world within the web of life. It must begin to invest the excess profits and wasted millions spent on advertising in the future of forestry and life on the planet. Carmanah Valley will never be logged!

Guardians of Life in the Ancient Forest
watercolor and ink
69 x 69 cm (27 1/2" x 27 1/2")

Catherine Moffat

Catherine Moffat's richly realistic work in watercolor, pastel, and pencil is fast gaining recognition. At her annual one-person exhibitions, most pieces are sold on the opening day to enthusiastic collectors who appreciate her skillful and sensitive approach to art. Still life makes up the major portion of her work, but her shows usually include a number of figure studies and landscapes. She is known for her versatility in artistic mediums as well as subject matter.

Over the past several years, her work has won a number of awards, including juror's choice awards in two regional juried exhibitions during 1988.

She has been invited to participate in an exhibition being mounted by Gallery 78 in Fredericton, New Brunswick, titled Artists of British Columbia, *in the company of many of this province's most prominent artists.*

Catherine Moffat lives in Victoria, British Columbia, where her work is represented by the Marshall Gallery.

The Carmanah Valley is not just big trees. It is an area so very beautiful and uplifting to experience that it is difficult to describe it with words that haven't been used repeatedly. Delicate trilliums nestle under mammoth spruce, and everywhere brilliant green leaves explode from the rich, russet earth. Forested hillsides climb up and up, fading into morning mist. The cool Carmanah Creek ripples pale green over smooth, gray stones, reflecting the surrounding forest in its deeper pools. All are part of an interconnected and interdependent whole.

Visiting a rainforest was a new experience for me, one that impressed me deeply. I gained new appreciation for how very grand nature can be when left to its own wisdom, left intact and treated with respect. It occurred to me many times while I was there that this area will never, ever exist again, if it is undermined by the effects of nearby logging.

Sharing the experience of Carmanah with a group of fellow artists, many of whom are dedicated and knowledgeable environmentalists, was an honor. We hiked, we painted, and we took pictures. We circled the evening fire, savoring hot chocolate, huge cookies, and lively conversation. Representing a wide diversity of mediums and philosophies, our common purpose was to capture the incredible natural beauty of this place, in the hope that our contributions of artwork would speak for the threatened Carmanah Valley, an irreplaceable treasure.

Our campsite on Carmanah Creek was very appropriately called Camp Heaven. About half a kilometre (one-third mile) from the camp, I encountered the scene illustrated opposite. I was drawn to the strong shapes and wanted to give the viewer an intimate sense of actually being within the forest.

Catherine Moffat

Close to Heaven
watercolor
52 x 52 cm (20½" x 20½")

François Mongeau

Born in 1946, François Mongeau has been sculpting since 1970. Although he spent a brief period at l'Ecole des Beaux Arts in Montreal, he is mostly self-taught. He worked for some months with Robert Davidson, a Haida artist, and became proficient with the native hooked knife and adze, as well as the traditional chisel and gouge.

A move to British Columbia started a whole new evolution for Mongeau. The creatures and people of the West Coast brought forth a new vista to be explored. He discovered the potential in driftwood. His sculpture, A Whale and Young, *carved from a nine-metre (thirty-foot) cedar log, stands as a landmark at French Creek on the Island Highway.*

In 1985/86 he returned to Quebec to study under master carver Roger André Bourgault at l'Ecole de Sculpture in St. Jean Port Joli. There, beginning with Mon Viel Ami, *Mongeau began a series of super-realistic visual poems, portraying the character in everyday apparel with subtle humor and integrity.*

With renewed enthusiasm, he returned to Vancouver Island and became part of the resident artist community at The Old School House Gallery in Qualicum Beach. Most recently, Mongeau has been working with weaver Elaine Duncan, producing unique carved and woven works that break traditional boundaries.

Mongeau's sculptures are in private collections in Europe and throughout North America.

Driving along logging roads, getting deeper into the wild, we pass clearcut after clearcut, eroded mountainsides, washed-out bridges. Finally, we arrive at our destination.

Down the trail we go. Slowly, we come to the tall trees—the giants of the forest. As we approach them, we seem to be getting smaller and a lot more humble. They have seen generations come and go for centuries. And here we are debating whether they should remain or not. What an absurd thought! For centuries they have sheltered plants, animals, and people, and lived in perfect harmony. How could anyone execute such a massacre?

As I walk among them, the light is ever-changing. The breeze sings through the branches in harmony with the song of birds. The moss under my feet is a living carpet. I come to a stream of fresh, clear water and drink; it fills me with vigor. This water would not be if it weren't for these trees; they are like the skin of the Earth.

After a day of peace, tranquility, and fresh air, we return to our car. With the smell of exhaust, the straightness of the road, and the bad news on the radio, we feel like returning to the forest. But responsibilities call us home, through miles of clear-cut devastation. It looks and feels like a war zone.

Only irresponsible people could create such devastation. Twenty years ago I came to Vancouver Island from Montreal. I was lost in this wilderness at first; I feared the unknown. Today I fear the city. May this preservation effort be successful and, like the roots of the forest, hold life secure for generations to come.

In *The Last Stand*, a grove of tall trees is surrounded by a clearcut and burn, so-called normal logging practice. An elder's face signifies the ancient continuity and permanence of nature rooted in the earth. Part of the circle, already broken, hangs by the roots. It is now or never that mankind must make the last stand in order to keep the Earth whole and alive.

The Last Stand
redcedar relief carving and mixed media
81 x 117 x 10 cm (32" x 46" x 4")

Douglas G. Morton

Born in 1926, in Winnipeg, Manitoba, Douglas G. Morton completed a year at the University of Manitoba before pursuing in earnest his interest in art. He studied at the Winnipeg School of Art under Lemoine Fitzgerald, the Art Centre School, the University of Southern California, the Académie Julian L'Ecole des Beaux-Arts, the studio of André L'Hôte in Paris, the Camberwell School of Art, the studio of Martin Bloch in London, and then at the Emma Lake Workshops in Saskatchewan.

Since 1950, he has been associated with a number of schools and universities in Canada. A professor and associate dean at York University in the early seventies, he became chairman of visual arts at the University of Victoria in 1988.

Morton has been included in a number of publications, including Contemporary Canadian Art, *published by Hurtig and the University of Toronto in 1983, and* Documents in Canadian Art, 1987. *He is represented in many corporate and private collections, as well as the Beaverbrook Art Gallery in Fredericton, New Brunswick; the National Gallery of Canada; the Art Gallery of Vancouver; and the Art Gallery of Greater Victoria.*

Morton's work has been exhibited extensively, including the opening exhibition at the National Gallery in Ottawa in 1988. In 1988-89 he visited the Stein Valley and contributed to A Celebration of Wilderness, *exhibited in Vancouver, Richmond, Kelowna, and Lillooet by the Western Canada Wilderness Committee.*

The difference in the ecological systems of the Stein and Carmanah valleys is striking—the Stein with its flourishing ponderosa pines contrasts with the rainforest environment which has nurtured the Sitka spruce in Carmanah.

It should be evident to everyone that our natural environment cannot tolerate for much longer the rapacious attitude toward nature that has been prevalent in this century. If we ignore the clear signals we are receiving, the humans on this planet will eventually cease to exist.

My 1989 print, *The Big Trees*, does not portray any specific aspect of the Carmanah Valley but deals with the profound beauty of the virgin forest. The symbolic forms I have used are the sun, old and new growth, and the paradox of coexistence or destruction.

This is the second print in my portfolio donated to the University of Victoria for its twenty-fifth anniversary celebration. In addition to the twenty-five prints in the edition, I produced six artist's proofs and eight studio proofs. All thirty-nine pieces were hand-pulled from hand-cut stencils to achieve the nineteen process colors.

I have portrayed the human image as a Chagall-type floating figure in the top left corner. The other elements, portraying old-growth, intermediate, and new-growth forest, are a combination of both Stein and Carmanah, with an overall theme of age, water, sun, and man. There is in all of nature a delicate balance of growth and decay; a natural order exists which must be respected. Our frantic pursuit of economic growth may prove to be suicidal if the land, sea, and air are the price that must be paid.

The Big Trees
silkscreen
60 x 44 cm (23½" x 17½")

Ryan Murraygreen

Ryan Murraygreen was born near Toronto, Ontario, in 1947. He received his B.A. in Oriental art history from the University of British Columbia and did graduate work at the UBC school of architecture and the Instituto Allende in Mexico.

He has received grants from the Canada Council and the Ontario Arts Council. Public exhibits of his work in paper can be found at the Cabrillo College Gallery in California, the Charles Scott Gallery in Vancouver, the Art Gallery of Hamilton in Ontario, the Capilano College Gallery in North Vancouver, and the San Francisco Museum of Modern Art.

He has taught and lectured at the University of British Columbia, Capilano College, the San Francisco Museum of Modern Art, the San Francisco Institute of Art, and the Vancouver Museum. A partial list of corporate and public collectors of his work includes Architectural Digest in Los Angeles, ten branches of Security Pacific Bank in California, B.C. Central Credit Union, Vancouver Museum, Bank of Puget Sound, Daon of Vancouver, Alcan of Vancouver and Montreal, Canada Development Corporation, and the Ledingham Design Group of Vancouver.

The lasting impression of my first visit to Carmanah Valley was the devastation of the clear-cut, burned war zone which is now the entrance to the tiny watershed. Carmanah is indeed a study in contrasts. First there is the blasted, burned, logged remains of a wilderness. Then comes the intense life and diversity of the old-growth forest: the huge cylindrical trunks disappearing into the forest canopy; the purple scaly bark of the giant spruce; the earth logs and encompassing vegetation.

Edward O. Wilson wrote: "The flora and fauna of a country become part of its natural heritage as important as its art and literature."

Collecting materials for paper-making from the plants in Carmanah, I was again reminded of the amazing artistic creations that are found in old-growth forests. Nothing man creates could ever contain the diversity of materials, texture, size, age (thousands of years), forms of life, and color that is found here. We cannot continue to compete with nature, looking at it from the human point of view only. If all of British Columbia is clear-cut, where will the wildlife retreat to? We must stop the destruction and learn to revere. We cannot substitute this diversity with tree plantations.

The devastation bordering Carmanah must serve as a warning. Civilization is a constant race between education and disaster. In whatever manner we can, we must all work to preserve the few remaining old-growth watersheds. Last year I was arrested for preventing mining in Strathcona Park. As an artist and a citizen, I feel privileged to participate in the efforts to preserve the greatest natural and national treasure we have, our old-growth forests.

R. Murraygreen

Aerial View Carmanah: River and Rainbow
handmade paper: cotton/old man's beard lichen/ bleached spruce roots/colored inks
64 x 41 cm (25" x 16")

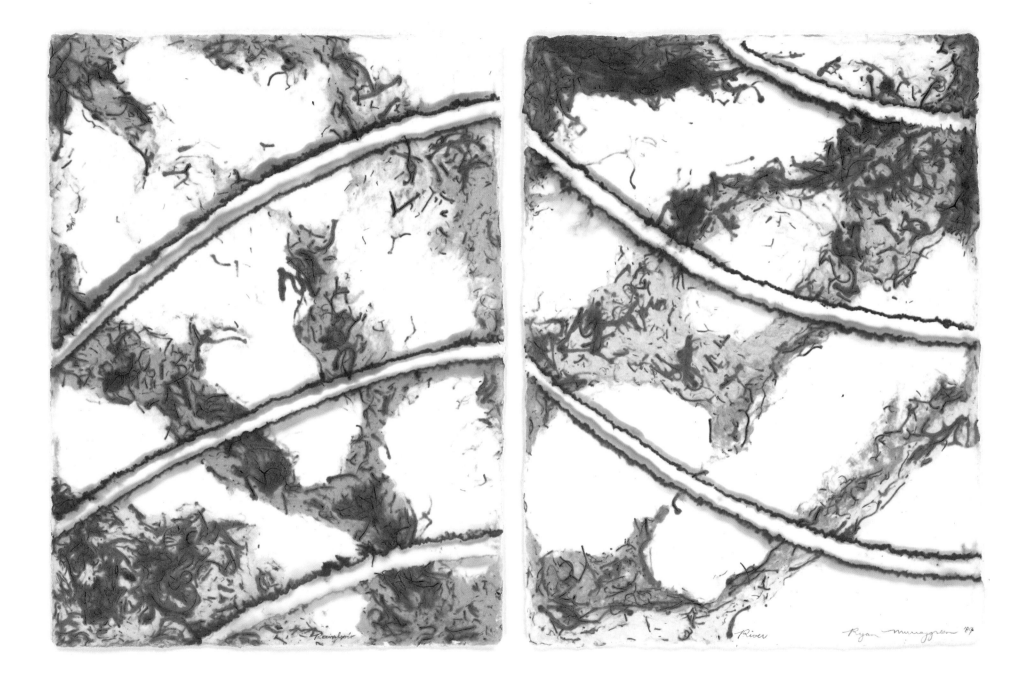

Rainlight   River   Ryan Murraygreen '87

Chris Nancarrow

Chris Nancarrow was born in England in 1926 and has been drawing all her life. She studied in wartime at the Central School of Art in London.

She married an Australian and lived in Sydney and Brisbane for many years, raising four children there. The decision to come to Canada in 1964 was partly influenced by seeing a traveling show of Inuit art, particularly the carvings: "fist-sized pieces of timeless and monumental impact." When her family had grown up, she studied sculpture and printmaking at the Kootenay School of Art.

During the seven years she worked as textile conservator at the Royal British Columbia Museum, she also studied Oriental brush technique with Stephen Sham, who influenced her more than any other teacher.

Her favorite works are in black and white by Goya, Hokusai, and Seurat; but, perceiving the universal hunger for color, she recently applied herself to using watercolor, often combined with pen and ink.

Now living on Vancouver Island, Nancarrow paints a broad range of subjects, including portraits.

I nearly didn't go to Carmanah. I was somewhat put off by the description of the ruggedness and there were interesting things happening at home. But a young friend said to me, "If they cut all the trees down, it will be important that every possible record is in existence, including yours." So I went to the valley and I was awed and grateful to be there.

The greens of the forest just blew my socks off, as did painting in the orderly chaos of growth-fighting-growth for the light.

All the artists I talked to felt as overwhelmed as I was. When someone suggested a preview by the creek of our first sketches, it was as if the heat had been turned up high under a simmering pot and our excitement rose and boiled over—a memorable experience in itself.

My feeling has all been joyful. I can't yet identify with the sense of outrage. I've seen a lot of outrage in my life, yet I still perceive a benevolent, wonderful system. Concentrating on the benevolence is a yeast that works.

I'm in some conflict about the best outcome we can hope for. I don't want to see tourists down here, or trails. (If that meant I hadn't seen it either, that would have been all

right.) Of course I don't want it butchered. I find myself saying, over and over, lines by nineteenth-century poet Gerard Manley Hopkins:

*What would the world be, once bereft
Of wet and of wildness? Let them
   be left,
O let them be left, wildness and wet;
Long live the weeds and the
   wilderness yet.*

Kitchen
watercolor
38 x 28 cm (15" x 11")

Nancarrow June 1989
Carruthers

Maxwell Newhouse

Maxwell Newhouse was born in Campbell River, British Columbia, in 1947. He excelled in art at school, and when only fifteen years old, he won first place for his poster publicizing the 1962 Nanaimo Music Festival.

In 1967, he began producing serious art. By 1969 he was accepted at the Vancouver School of Art (now the Emily Carr College of Art and Design) as a third-year student because of his advanced grasp of contemporary movements and the volume of work he had completed. A year later the law firm of MacIsaac, Sinclair and Clark asked him to create an original painting for a project of growing roots over geometric forms.

During the seventies he participated in a number of shows: Discoveries 1971 *at the Burnaby Art Gallery; a two-man show with Drew Burnham, titled* History Makers, *at Avelles Gallery; a one-man show,* Four Seasons of the Canadian Flag, *at the Equinox Gallery; and* Artist and His Collection *at the Victoria Art Gallery. In 1974, at the Vancouver Art Gallery, he performed* Concerto With Sledgehammer and Concrete *and exhibited a set of conceptual drawings.*

Today he continues to produce, expanding on the concept of using the Canadian flag as inspiration, creating hundreds of works, waiting and looking for the right time and place to exhibit.

I am seeing so many things slip away in my lifetime. We just have to save this bit of forest. It's like a chapel—some kind of a holy shrine. It is something old, something beautiful, and it gives me a sense of timelessness.

I've always been considered a bit odd with my work, although I do paint—very seriously and rigorously. I once did a piece in Vancouver called *Concerto with Sledgehammer and Concrete*. I mounted a concrete slab and the performance took a minute at the very most. All I did was attack the slab. It flew everywhere and the critics all ran out of the room. It was quite wild—very successful—and better than any painting I've done. I had drawings all around, which the critics liked, but I like my art to be real.

The *Carmanah Jewel Project* is to be started in 1990 and finished in 2350. A ring is to be constructed of stainless steel, the inside made solid with concrete to prevent the roots from crushing the ring when growing. Near Rosander Main, just a two-minute walk from the road in an existing clearcut next to the Carmanah Valley, the ground will be raised and made level and the ring completely buried. At this point, professionals will supervise the planting of nine trees above the ring. All around the ring, a meadow will remain clear for about thirty metres (one hundred feet) from the new tree line. In the beginning the project will have to be serviced every five years for approximately fifty years, then every ten years for the next one hundred years, then every twenty years for two hundred years. Each time the ground level will be lowered a little. Finally, when this very heavy ring is completely exposed and supported in the year 2350, the steel will be buffed shiny and the land returned to its original contour. This project at 360 years old will be considered complete, shining like a jewel, a gift from the twentieth century.

The Carmanah Jewel Project
conceptual piece,
watercolor rendering by Drew Burnham
52 x 51 cm (20 1/2" x 20")

Mark Nyhof

Mark Nyhof was born in Victoria, British Columbia, in 1958. A keen naturalist, he has combined his interest in wildlife with his skill as an artist. Using watercolors and gouache, Nyhof's paintings focus primarily on birds as subjects, with only hints of their environment. Paying attention to detail, he ensures that there are no distractions caused by inaccuracy. His ultimate goal, however, is to try and capture the personality of a particular species, or the mood of a situation as he remembers it from his observations in the wild.

Nyhoff presently works out of his Victoria studio. Recently, one of his paintings was part of the traveling exhibition, Profiles of a Heritage, *organized by the Centennial Wildlife Society of British Columbia. Another of his paintings was selected for the prestigious* Birds in Art *exhibition this fall at the Leigh Yawkey Woodson Art Museum in Wausau, Wisconsin.*

Upon seeing the Carmanah Valley for the first time this summer, I was overwhelmed by its beauty and most impressed by the size of the trees. They were not just big, they were huge. A group of enormous Sitka spruce at Camp Heaven and another group just to the north were particularly memorable.

The forest is truly nature at its finest. The perfect balance of all elements has produced something quite remarkable—something worth saving for its own sake, and also for ourselves and future generations. Those who have not been to the valley and find it difficult to understand should go and stand in the forest as I did, then make the drive back through the nearby clearcuts. The contrast is startling. Without seeing the valley, it's hard to imagine what was once there.

My painting, *Barred Owl*, is of one of the many owl species that occur in the Carmanah Valley. In British Columbia, the barred owl, like its counterpart the spotted owl, has historically been found in mature forests. Recently, both species have been severely affected by loss of habitat due to logging.

After a forest is logged, the clearcuts and even the second-growth timber fall well short of providing the basic requirements for these owls. Both barred and spotted owls nest in the hollows created when the tops or branches of large old-growth trees break off. Unfortunately, most second-growth trees are not large enough to satisfy their nesting requirements. As well, roost sites, which provide necessary concealment and adequate protection from heat during daylight hours, are not readily available in second-growth forest. The barred owl has proven to be quite adaptable, expanding its range considerably in recent years. Many forests that did not previously have barred owls now do—possibly at the expense of other owl species. The less aggressive spotted owl has not adapted well and its numbers are now at a critical low.

Barred Owl
watercolor
27 x 33 cm (10½" x 13")

Toni Onley

Toni Onley was born in 1928 on the Isle of Man where he received his early art training and was influenced by the work of the great British watercolorists. He came to Canada in 1948, living first in Ontario, then moving to British Columbia in 1955.

In 1957, with scholarships to the Instituto Allende in Mexico, he came under the influence of abstract expressionism. His significant painting began in Mexico, where he remained for three years. Returning to Vancouver in 1958, he was offered an exhibition at the Vancouver Art Gallery. The early sixties were a fertile period of exploration and solidification of direction for him.

Winning a senior Canada Council fellowship in 1963, he studied etching in London, England, and re-established his landscape roots with the Norwich School of Watercolor Painting. His course was now set toward the work he is best known for today: landscapes of simplicity and power. His paintings capture the essence of specific moments in time, the presence of objects, and relationships of color, light and shadow.

Public collections include: Tate Gallery, London, England; Victoria and Albert Museum, London, England; National Gallery of Canada; Seattle Art Museum; Vancouver Art Gallery; the Library of Congress, Washington D.C.; and the Art Gallery of Greater Victoria.

I am sitting in my studio contemplating a wood sample from a yellow-cedar over one thousand years old. It was cut down on Graham Island in the Queen Charlotte archipelago in 1985 and left behind to rot in the course of normal clear-cut logging. I count the rings in for five centimetres (two inches) from its bark and come to the year 1808, the year that Simon Fraser reached the mouth of the Fraser River. I continue to count inwards for a further twenty-two centimetres (nine inches) and come to the year 1497, the year that John Cabot discovered Canada's east coast. Already this yellow-cedar was an ancient tree that had been growing undisturbed for over five hundred years.

Likewise, Carmanah Valley's rainforest contains some of the world's oldest living things. But to the logging industry, they represent a very limited supply of wood. Left to stand, they are an eternal vision, a creation that surpasses art. The valley has the world's tallest Sitka spruce at 95 metres (312 feet). This tree and all the other giants that populate the Carmanah Valley had the misfortune to begin life in a country that would eventually become Canada. Had they grown in Japan, their great girth would now be bound by sacred ropes. Incense would climb into their lofty peaks from temples dedicated to longevity.

My answer to the logging industry's slogan of "Share the Forest" is that it has had its share. It is now time to stop and take an inventory of what little of the first-growth forest is left to us and future generations and to consider how we can make the very best use of it. In the few days I spent painting among these cathedral spires, I met people who had come from as far away as Russia to see them. They will continue to come from all over the world for as long as the great trees stand.

I do not want to see another wood sample on my studio wall, this time from a giant of the Carmanah Valley, mounted for display on a thank-you plaque. In this fight, there are no winners and losers—we will all lose.

toni onley

Morning Fog, Carmanah Valley
watercolor
38 x 28 cm (15" x 11")

Morning fog. Carmanah Valley, B.C. 7 May 1989   onley

Ron Parker

Ron Parker was born December 4, 1942, in Vancouver, British Columbia, where he graduated in 1960 from Lord Byng High School. His educational background is diverse; he holds a B. Ed. degree from the University of British Columbia, but also studied commercial art and architecture.

He began painting wildlife in 1978, and his first one-man show, held in Vancouver, was an instant sell-out. Since then he has had numerous gallery shows throughout Canada and the United States.

Parker and his art have been featured in many publications, including Outdoor Canada, Wildlife Art News, Midwest Art, *and* Art Impressions. *He was also one of twelve artists highlighted in* From the Wild, *published by Summerhill Press in 1986. Over ninety of his paintings have been reproduced by Mill Pond Press of Florida.*

He lives in Courtenay, British Columbia, with his wife, Maureen, and his two daughters, Kimberly and Allison.

Unusual hikes in unique environments are inspirational for me, and the Carmanah Valley has both. The hike down the canyon from Camp Heaven to the Carmanah Giant is physically enjoyable, its ladders and steep sections requiring some exertion. With the old-growth forest on each bank and the creek below crashing over small falls, flowing swiftly over rocky flats, or lying in deep green pools, it becomes spectacular. Hikers can view towering thousand-year-old cedars or five-hundred-year-old Sitka spruce from different altitudes, depending on trail elevation along the steep canyon sides.

The spruce groves have a quiet majesty that invites you to stay awhile. This is not a place to hurry through but a place to linger and enjoy the melodious call of a thrush or the raucous chatter of a Steller's jay.

In places you can see where a fallen giant Sitka spruce, perhaps five hundred years old, has become a nurse log for huge hemlocks, themselves three hundred or more years old, now arranged in a straight line with their uppermost roots exposed. You can look back eight hundred or more years in time here.

Europeans may view their ancient buildings and structures as their roots in antiquity but we, as West Coast North Americans, can look upon our old-growth forests as our literal roots in antiquity.

I sincerely hope that some complete valleys of old-growth forest will be preserved as our national heritage for the enjoyment of our children. Let's start with saving Carmanah.

Black-tailed Deer in Sitka Spruce
acrylic on masonite
71 x 36 cm (28" x 14")

Brad Piatka

Born in Port Alberni, British Columbia, in 1957, Brad Piatka displayed an early interest in art, drawing recognizable pictures at age two. In 1964, he spent three years in Lestock, Saskatchewan, returned to Port Alberni, then spent a year in Campbell River, British Columbia, where a sketch pad and pencil were his constant companions. For the next four years he lived in the tiny logging camp of Kokish, British Columbia, where his interest and ability in art grew. A final move returned him to Port Alberni.

At age eighteen, he began painting in oils while working as a logger. His first public show was held in Port Alberni in 1976. Painting remained a hobby for ten years, until he entered Port Alberni's fall fair juried art show. He won first and second prize for The Grass Cap *and* Cougar *and overall best in show, winning again at the Nanaimo regional juried art show.* The Grass Cap *was selected for the B.C. Festival of the Arts in Prince George, British Columbia, and chosen to hang at the Robson Square Media Centre, representing the Expo pavilion.*

Piatka continues to show his paintings. No stranger to the West Coast, nor to the canvas, he is able to depict its natural settings with such enthusiasm that the outcome is the next best thing to being there.

When a person listens carefully to the issues involving the Carmanah Valley and its possible future, it is easy to make a decision to save it or log it, depending on where you stand.

Yet, after visiting the Carmanah, the reality of its pristine beauty and ensuing destruction has even greater impact. It is no longer just a place you've heard about. It is a place you've spent time in and marveled at.

As an artist, my first priority is to attempt to capture beautiful places such as the Carmanah on canvas, yet I have also earned a living as a logger for seven years. I believe this gives me a certain amount of insight into both sides of this particular issue. Unfortunately, it only seems to make it harder to come to any definite conclusions.

I believe that both sides of this issue must be fully represented in order that neither side has too much or too little control.

I am not at this time an active lobbyist for preservation, but I am very sensitive to and aware of the fact that the need is growing. Our forest industry, with the jobs that it provides, is what brings us here and allows us to stay in British Columbia. Yet the beauty is what allows us to enjoy and be proud of our province. The Carmanah is a grand example of what we have to be proud of.

Brad Piatka

The Triad
oil
64 x 102 cm (25" x 40")

126

Renée Poisson

Renée Poisson began drawing and painting as a teenager. She received a B.A. in philosophy from the University of British Columbia in 1964, then moved to California to study and work with Marguerite Wildenhain, an early graduate of Bauhaus. After travelling for two years in Europe and North Africa, Poisson moved to Philadelphia and began working with clay. She taught there until 1969.

She was subsequently drawn back to the west coast of Vancouver Island, eventually becoming part of a loosely knit community of artists living on Long Beach. She constructed a wood-fired kiln and built a pottery wheel, working with clay from the banks along the shoreline. In 1971, she sailed in the South Pacific and spent a year in the New Hebrides, drawing, painting, and print-making. Returning to Vancouver Island, she began homesteading in Merville, 300 kilometres (180 miles) north of Victoria, in 1977. She owns and operates a nursery specializing in heritage fruit trees.

Sculpture has been her language for over twenty years. She began with clay and moved to wood as her primary medium. She is surrounded by her work, having populated the forest with Sentinels and Guardians—carved and painted figures up to three metres (ten feet) tall, which possess the qualities of humor, frailty, strength, and triumph.

This is the first time I've had the opportunity of contributing as an artist to saving some of our wilderness. Art is important because a work comes so strongly from the artist that it can be a challenging experience for the viewers. Something might catch their attention and make them stop—allowing consciousness a new space. They might not understand it; it doesn't matter if they like it or not. By shifting a little, a gap is left for some of their own feelings to surface, freed from their usual boundaries. I am optimistic that if people could open up just a bit, they would see and be aware of the whole planet. They would know that we are creatures of it; it is part of us and part of who we are.

The trail I took in the valley was like a sculpture. I walked on fallen trees that were all beautifully terraced and textured. As I went from one to another, there were little railings and ropes. It was so amazing that I just wanted to keep walking, on and on. I ended up feeling completely dizzy, high, elated, but very respectful too.

It is really important for the logging here to stop. I was shocked by the millions of tonnes of wood left on the clear-cut area, and by the devastation of the soil. If we managed our forests well, we could produce the wood we need and still have the wilderness.

Hearing the chainsaws as I walked along the river, I pictured the hillsides logged. It would no longer be wilderness, that's all. The hand of man would be extremely visible. I think people's sanity depends on being able to really be back in the primeval womb.

The sculpture, made of branches from the clearcut above the trailhead, is my personal ode to the strength, beauty, and frailty of the forests of the earth, with which we humans are inextricably united.

Carmanah
cedar and hemlock branches,
river gravel, graphite, and bronze pins
76 x 218 x 64 cm (30" x 86" x 25")

Don Radcliffe

Don Radcliffe was born in a small mining village in Scotland called Calderbank, where he attended the local school. When his mother died, he moved to Glasgow. At Morrison's Academy Boarding School, he became very interested in art. The winner of a school art exhibit, he was given a scholarship to the Scottish School of Art.

His artistic gift remained dormant during the twelve years he spent with the British Merchant Marines, traveling all over the world, seeing how people lived, their homes, and their countries. His painting began again in 1963, when he completed three watercolors.

In 1970, he moved to Sechelt, British Columbia, rented a cottage on the beach, and started painting. After a year, he started a successful fishing charter business which he ran for five years. Returning to Vancouver, he had various jobs, including marina manager and boat salesman. Radcliffe started painting again full time in 1980. He has had several exhibits and sold paintings in Scotland, England, Wales, France, Africa, Australia, Japan, and China. He now owns the Leafhill Gallery in Victoria, British Columbia, and continues to paint as much as possible.

I believe strongly that we should keep things for our children. Most of the people who are doing the logging have immediate plans in mind, and I don't blame them for that. They've got to feed their families—their children—but they're not looking ahead. There won't be anything for anyone to see in fifty years if they continue what they're doing. I don't think it's right. If I had the money I'd buy the whole valley and make sure they didn't do it.

It's a good thing for a group of artists to get together. The musicians amazed me when they contributed to a musical extravaganza all over the world. They made a tremendous amount of money. If we all got together, not just artists, but all the people who are concerned, who can think a little bit ahead—five, ten, twenty-five years—it would make a big difference.

I'm not a youngster anymore and I'd like to make a really strong statement. I'd like to paint a hill that has been clear-cut, with nothing on it but stumps and slash, and in the front of it I would like to put a glass case with a sapling in it and call it *The Last Sapling, Compliments of MacMillan Bloedel.* People must be shocked into seeing what is happening. I want to say to them, "Look, this is what they are doing—to your country. This is what your children are going to see—all these bare hills."

Now, you've seen a lot of paintings, you've seen a lot of beautiful things in your life. Go to the Carmanah Valley and see it as it really is. It's absolutely beautiful.

No Place to Nest
watercolor
53 x 36 cm (21" x 14")

Michael R. Semkiw

Mike Semkiw was born in Port Alberni, British Columbia, in 1961. By the time he graduated from high school, he knew he wanted to pursue a close association with nature. The next few years were spent studying wildlife on his own while working for various fish hatcheries and with the Department of Fisheries and Oceans in British Columbia's coastal waters. This experience allowed him to observe his subjects in their natural environment.

Semkiw is mainly self-taught and believes in trying to show each species as accurately as possible, paying close attention to details. He believes in versatility as an artist, sometimes creating problems for himself, but ultimately solving them. He has worked with a variety of mediums, including graphite, charcoal, pastels, gouache, pen and ink, tempera, silk-screen, printing, photography, leather, metal-etching, pottery, clay sculpture, and carvings in wood, sandstone, soapstone, and argillite. Presently, he mainly works with watercolors, acrylics, and oils.

Involved with nature and art since he was a child, Semkiw finds himself becoming more alarmed and concerned with environmental issues. He has begun a book of paintings on the rare and endangered species of Canada. With a number of private commissions behind him, he is developing into a serious wildlife artist with a goal of being discovered internationally.

There aren't too many places left where you can hike around and see things as substantial and as impressive as this. This whole valley is unique. I've been trying to list all the different species of wildlife and plants. There are so many things here to paint. I could spend a year here and still not get it all done.

I support total preservation of the valley. I'm concerned that if they only save a small section, the wind will take more and more out each year because the buffer isn't big enough. The trees will fall. I'm concerned too, about the life-forms in the river. Everything will be damaged.

Turning Back

No longer shall I live in illusion,
For now I seek my due seclusion,
Where I can feel the essence of
    past
And put present pains to rest,
    alas!

So close I've come, I near forgot
The beauty which can never be
    bought:
To see raw nature at her best,
Birds and animals put to the test.

There is no room for trial or error
In these vast lands—only terror.
Only the strong will ever strive
While the weak shall not survive.

This is a place where one can touch
Cool mountain streams that hold
    so much.
They start with a trickle from far
    and high
But soon they gather and rage on by.

The massive spires towering green
Blanket slopes where wildlife
    teem.
Somewhere in time I hope to find
A better understanding and peace
    of mind.

For maybe then will man truly see
My passion for nature comes from
    sincerity.
I hope and pray our thoughts will
    become clear
So we can erase all thoughts of fear.

Mike Semkiw

Forest Dweller
acrylic and watercolor
32 x 40 cm (12½" x 15½")

Jack Shadbolt

Jack Shadbolt is a Canadian artist widely known both at home and abroad. An exhibitor of long experience, he has represented Canada in many traveling art shows. He has been for many years a teacher, lecturer, and writer, exerting a large influence as an advocate of contemporary art. He is widely represented in both public and private collections.

Shadbolt has been the subject of several retrospective exhibitions, including a thirty-year exhibit at the National Gallery of Canada. He received the Canadian section International Guggenheim Award in 1957 and a Canadian government overseas fellowship on which he worked in France, Italy, and Greece. He has traveled extensively.

Shadbolt has executed several mural commissions, including works for the Edmonton International Airport and the National Arts Centre in Ottawa. He received the Order of Canada in 1972 and is the recipient of honorary university degrees. His honors include the Molson Award, the Ontario Society of Artists award, and the University of Alberta Award for the Arts. He was also recently made a freeman of the city of Vancouver.

He is the author of three books on the artist's creative process: In Search of Form, Mind's I *(poems and drawings) and* Act of Art, *all published by McClelland and Stewart. A comprehensive book on fifty years of his work will be published in the fall of 1990 by Douglas & McIntyre.*

Going into the Carmanah Valley was a nostalgic experience for me, recalling my younger days when I used to visit Emily Carr and see her paintings of brooding forest interiors. The titanic root systems and the trees out-towering the mind at Carmanah are an overwhelming experience.

Vancouver Island is a magnificent natural heritage that should be carefully cherished and not be allowed to be indiscriminately destroyed by industrial depredation. The world needs such places for its environmental and recreational well-being. I'm sure that in the long run the preservation of such natural wonders as Carmanah will attract visitors to British Columbia whose peripheral tourist-spending will considerably more than outweigh the temporary profits of clear-cut logging.

The importance of such symbols as Carmanah to the imaginative wonder of our lives cannot be overestimated. Our increasing drift toward megalopolitan city cultures with their materialistic attitudes and competitive tensions makes it imperative for sanity's sake that images of wild, untouched nature be available for our relaxation of spirit.

And if we must be practical, a relaxed people place less stress on the costly social welfare systems. I see people in here camping with kids who will have memories that will never desert them. We have enough people in institutions nowadays who sit staring at the wall—people who haven't anything in their memories to hold them and sustain them. Anything which nourishes the spirit is worth preserving.

I think it makes good common, clear sense to hang on right now and fight hard to preserve what's left of this wilderness.

Jack Shadbolt

Carmanah Valley
graphite on paper
72 x 87 cm (28 1/4″ x 34″)

Jan Sharkey-Thomas

A Canadian by choice, Jan Sharkey-Thomas was born in the Hudson Valley in 1930 and grew up in Yonkers, New York. Her father, a freelance illustrator, led her through the paths of conventional mediums. After a formal art education in Manhattan, she freelanced there commercially. In 1963, she immigrated to Ontario, happy to find grass without candy wrappers, people who didn't shove, and mink and ermine worn by the animals that were born with these skins.

She became actively interested in the World Wildlife Fund and other conservation movements in the late sixties after rescuing an adult ocelot and becoming aware of the consequences of the exotic pet trade. The cat has been her companion and model for more than twenty years.

The major thrust of Sharkey-Thomas's work has been animal and wilderness themes. Her originals were reproduced by Pepper House Fine Arts of Ottawa, from 1969 to 1985. She has had solo exhibitions most years since 1972, usually in Ontario, and two in New York. British Columbia lured her for the ten years she assisted Clarence Tillenious with wildlife drawing classes at the Okanagan Summer School of the Arts, and she is now a permanent resident of Saltspring Island. Her three sons, Antony, Ethan, and Paul Marcano, are all Gulf Island artists as well.

Visitors to the ancient forest in Carmanah Valley are not likely to come away untouched. This is a place of extraordinary beauty: nature as herself, wondrously creative, patient, and tenacious. More than that, the past is bound to the present in a very special way. Centuries of our continent's history linger in the cores of giant spruce, while new life flourishes on the moist, rich floor, lush with ferns. The very same trees that marked the paths of the original inhabitants are guiding similar trails for us. When we circle one great tree, we know that generation after generation has evolved in that same presence.

In the shadows of such timelessness, I feel like little more than a butterfly. It is easy to understand what native people mean when they speak of sharing the forest with everything that lives in it. That kind of harmony is glowingly evident; a borrowing and returning of energy, a symbiotic blending of forms and levels and ages of life. In this magic place, a tree feels like a brother, with a knowledge of its own.

To experience this setting as an artist, to try to interpret it for someone else, is a curious challenge. The scale alone is staggering; no canvas is tall or broad enough. It is so much more than just what we can see. It is something very fundamental that grips all the senses at once; it is a bond with the Earth—a feeling that can't be drawn, painted, or crafted. But images will emerge for all of us and will be revelations in themselves.

The denseness of the forest mutes the sound of logging machinery working all around us, but the drone is searing in its purpose. As I walk the mossy aisles between towering velvet arches, I cannot tell myself that this is only "board feet" and jobs for Canada. How can we think of continuing to devour such an exquisite master plan—and even imagine that we can survive when we have finished with it? And the trees themselves? They stand in silence right beside us, elegant, mighty—and utterly defenceless.

J. Sharkey Thomas

Forest Ghosts
oil on canvas
92 x 122 cm (36" x 48")

Arnold Shives

Arnold Shives was born in Vancouver, British Columbia, in 1943. After two years at the University of British Columbia studying art history, he enroled at the San Francisco Art Institute, receiving a B.F.A. in painting in 1966. From 1966 to 1968 he studied at Stanford University on a Carnegie Corporation fellowship and received an M.A. in painting.

He has long been involved in printmaking and painting, and his work has been exhibited overseas and throughout Canada. A number of museums have acquired Shives's work for their collections: the Edmonton Art Gallery, the Winnipeg Art Gallery, the Achenbach Foundation, California Palace of the Legion of Honor, the New York Public Library, and the National Gallery of Canada.

He has received a number of awards, including several from the Canada Council, and in 1988 was chosen to join the Octogon expedition of artists to the Comox Glacier and the Celebration of Wilderness expedition to the Stein Valley.

A wilderness enthusiast, he derives inspiration for his art from British Columbia's spectacular scenery. His concern for the environment is a natural outcome of his years as a mountaineer, when he climbed in rugged and remote areas of the coastal mountains.

I recall ocean mist penetrating the valley in the morning and retreating under the high spring sun. It seemed to bear the message, "pacific," and the river echoed in response: "tranquility, tranquility." There is something about the softness, the ambience of this valley—the way the light is filtered and softened. It is a beautiful place.

The masters of the rainforest, the Sitka spruce, cluster in groves, rising like craggy pinnacles, decked in trailing moss and ferns. They inspire awe, thrusting upwards nearly 100 metres (330 feet). Spiky, great-girthed cedars, with sinuous draping branches, have stood rooted on the Carmanah hillsides for the better part of a millennium.

I was aware the valley was threatened because I could hear the grinding of logging equipment up the hill—reminding me that this is a very small place. We're not talking about saving an immense area, just a postage-stamp-sized piece of wilderness. I don't think it's an unreasonable request that this small ecosystem be saved.

Many authorities have raised the alarm regarding the depletion of our forests. I find pertinent these words of Pope John Paul II: "In the horizon of faith the Earth is no undiminished reservoir to be exploited, but is part of the mystery of creation... The human person often seems to see no other meaning in the natural environment than what serves for immediate use and consumption. Yet it was the Creator's will that we should communicate with nature as intelligent guardians and not as heedless exploiters and destroyers."

It is my hope that we may re-acquire a spirit, an attitude of wonder—and a good place to do so is on the banks of the unspoiled Carmanah Creek.

Arnold Shives

Rainforest—Carmanah Creek
monotype
71 x 96 cm (28" x 38")

Gordon Smith

Born in Sussex, England, in 1919, Gordon Smith moved to Manitoba in 1934. He enroled at the Winnipeg School of Art, under Lionel Lemoine Fitzgerald, and began teaching children's art classes.

After four years in the Princess Patricia's Canadian Light Infantry and a war wound, he enroled in the Vancouver School of Art (now the Emily Carr College of Art and Design) and in 1946 taught graphics and design there. Between 1946 and 1957, he took courses at the California School of Fine Arts and studied at Harvard University. In 1956 Smith joined the University of British Columbia, where he taught for twenty-six years.

Smith has received numerous awards and commissions, including an honorary doctorate from Simon Fraser University, first prizes in the Biennial of Canadian Art from the National Gallery of Canada in 1955, the Canadian Group, Montreal, in 1968, and the Royal Canadian Architectural Institute allied arts medal. He has done works for the Queen Elizabeth Theatre and Simon Fraser University in Vancouver; the Law Library of the University of Western Ontario; the Canadian Trade Pavilion in Tokyo; the Canadian Pavilion at the 1970 World's Fair in Osaka, Japan; and the Canadian Embassy, Washington, D. C. in 1988.

Smith is represented in numerous corporate, museum, and art gallery collections in Canada, the United States, England, Wales, and Switzerland.

From my early childhood in the south of England, I have been influenced by walks in the country, the South Downs, and seeing the landscapes of the British Romantic painters, including Blake and Samuel Palmer among others. Later I was stimulated by the painting of the Abstract Expressionists of the late forties, and more recently, I discovered the paintings of Goya, Courbet, Monet, and Soutine. For the last few years my images have been a struggle to balance the act of painting and the landscape.

For me, seeing the forest in the Carmanah Valley was one of the most deeply moving experiences I have had. It is easy to sound romantic about this, but just like visiting the ancient Haida sites on the Queen Charlotte Islands, this was a more religious experience than attending a service in a great cathedral.

Walking through this forest, seeing, feeling, touching, and hearing . . . giant spruces growing straight and tall . . . tangled undergrowth of sword fern and huckleberry . . . sweet forest smells . . . the softness of moss clinging to branches . . . ancient gnarled stumps . . . ravens . . . eagles . . . small birds singing in the underbrush.

Seeing and feeling these things with gentle and concerned friends who share similar feelings are all part of my experience of the Carmanah Valley.

The Tree, Carmanah Forest, is a departure from the direction my work is taking today. The image had an overwhelming impact on my senses. This is my homage to the subject—the tree itself being more important than the act of painting and the artist.

Gordon A Smith

The Tree, Carmanah Forest
acrylic
115 x 92 cm (45" x 36¼")

Peggy Sowden

Peggy's love of painting and wild places began as a child. Always encouraged by her mother, a landscape painter, to stop, look, understand, and interpret what she saw, Peggy developed an early appreciation for the art process. Her father, an avid outdoorsman, took her family into the wilds of British Columbia and from these summer adventures, seeds were sown for a love of wilderness. Sowden studied visual and performing arts in high school, worked as a naturalist, entered fine art school, and became a veterinarian caring for injured wildlife; the two interests of art and nature are interwoven in a lifelong passion.

Seated on the forest floor, drawing, I am humbled by the towering trees. These enormous spruce seem to stand as monuments to time, giving me a sense of history and place. Living alongside of man, they bear silent witness to our failings and our triumphs. In their presence, I am reminded of the extraordinary natural world that exists inexorably intertwined with mine.

There is a special light created in an old-growth forest—a soft, filtered light which seems to make objects glow. The air is quiet and in the stillness I am at ease.

As custodians of the ancient watersheds of the west coast of Vancouver Island, we have a decision to make. Do we convert the rainforest to barren ground, waiting years for it to be covered by cultured trees, exchanging the irreplaceable giants for second growth? Or do we pass along to the next generation the gift only an old forest can give?

Carmanah Valley is a fine example of a living natural museum, a unique dynamic forest storing diverse genetic secrets. Left intact, it will provide inspiration for everyone who enters for many generations. Old-growth forests are disappearing throughout the world.

We have far fewer places where we can be close to nature, nature untouched by man. Are we in such desperate economic need that we must rob future generations of their choices?

Peggy Sowden

Growing Skyward
watercolor on paper
38 x 56 cm (15" x 22")

George Steggles

George Steggles was born in London, England. After service in the Royal Air Force, he was a full-time student for five years at Hornsey College of Art.

After graduating with a national diploma in painting and an art teacher's diploma from London University, he spent twelve years as a specialist art teacher in London high schools.

The following five years were spent as a senior lecturer at Brighton College of Education in Sussex. He immigrated to Canada in 1967 to take up the post of associate professor at the University of Manitoba's faculty of education.

Steggles was a member of the art education department at the University of Victoria from 1980 until his early retirement as associate professor emeritus in 1988.

Since coming to the West Coast, he has developed a strong interest in painting the landscape, and this has led to increasing admiration for the work of painters such as Tom Thomson and the Group of Seven.

He is a frequent exhibitor in Victoria and his work is represented in collections in Canada, England, and Greece. His recent work reflects a growing fascination with the problems of relating the human figure to the landscape.

I welcomed the opportunity to visit the Carmanah Valley in June, 1989. As one of a group of artists hosted by the Western Canada Wilderness Committee, I am left with vivid memories, along with a strong sense of shock and foreboding.

After the long, hot, dusty, and extremely depressing journey through miles of devastated landscape above Nitinat Lake, it was a relief to enter the forest at the trailhead. This feeling was heightened when, after an hour of backpacking down a fairly steep trail, we emerged at the campsite by Carmanah Creek. It was as though we had stumbled upon an oasis—a sort of west coast Shangri-La.

The Carmanah fully lives up to its reputation. It is impossible not to be affected by the sheer majesty of the forest and by the overwhelming sense of peace and tranquility.

The next two days were filled with the familiar and pleasurable activities of sketching and making notes, but the technical problems of conveying even a hint of these visual splendors were formidable. I found it extremely difficult to confront such an emotionally charged landscape and then give adequate expression to the experience. I was still haunted by visions of the ravaged mountains above the valley. I could still taste the choking dust of that shattered landscape through which we would have to return.

Early on the second day, the shocking reality of the situation became clear to me. I was attempting to do some sort of artistic justice to a magnificent grove of spruce trees. Gradually I became aware of a muffled sound echoing through the forest—an insistent grinding and growling of machinery almost overhead, it seemed.

It was Monday—another working day—and the clear-cutting juggernauts were poised upon the very brink of the Carmanah Valley.

My painting concentrates on a high point of the event itself, rather than trying to convey the horror I feel over this appalling situation. A key moment in the whole emotional experience was the tremendous sense of relief I felt as we left a hideous wasteland and entered the lush and welcoming forest.

Artists on the Trail
oil on panel
55 x 61 cm (21$\frac{1}{2}$" x 23$\frac{3}{4}$")

Carole Thompson

Carole Thompson lives in Courtenay, British Columbia, and teaches painting at Arts Umbrella in Vancouver. She was born in 1945 in Barrie, Ontario, and graduated from Vancouver School of Art (now the Emily Carr College of Art and Design) in 1967. Since then, she has shown her work in many galleries, including the Surrey Art Gallery, Burnaby Art Gallery, Bau-Xi Gallery, Vancouver Art Gallery, and the Art Gallery of Greater Victoria. Her work is represented in several public collections, including Simon Fraser University; Esso Resources Collection, Calgary; Mercantile Bank, Vancouver; Canada Council Art Bank, Ottawa; and numerous private collections in Canada and the United States.

Wilderness should not have to justify its preservation. It has to be protected and nurtured for the future just because it exists. I place a very high value on the concept of wilderness preservation; it is important that some areas of this planet be left relatively untouched by outside influences. Even if I cannot visit these areas personally, just to know they are there is enough.

The Carmanah Valley and other wilderness areas give us in North America a particular kind of heritage. Like the architecture and medieval cities of Europe, our wilderness contains a lot of history. This forest is a very ancient one and would be absolutely impossible to duplicate.

We can use the Carmanah Valley as a place to study and learn about the interconnectedness of all life forms—including man. Every day it becomes more evident that there is a strong interdependence between us and our environment.

I would like to see the Carmanah Valley preserved in honor and appreciation of one of the most beautiful places left on the Earth.

The spiritual presence, one of the qualities found in the Carmanah Valley, has to be personally experienced.

It is my hope that in the future many other people will also be able to experience the peacefulness and aura of protection that this ancient forest provides.

Carole Thompson

Dreams of Carmanah
mixed media
65 x 102 cm (25½″ x 40½″)

Diana Thompson

Diana Thompson is a West Coast native who has always had a strong connection to the world of nature. As a teenager, even when friends and the snow-clad ski hills beckoned, she preferred to spend her time bird-watching. Her friends knew her as a hopeless romantic; a birdwatcher; impossible.

In university she didn't stand out so much from the crowd. The biology professors urged her on, promising her a future in fungi. The art department sighed and suggested that dead birds were far more interesting than live ones. She liked both, and flourished. She was a park naturalist, a first-class student, an illustrator, and a grateful recipient of awards. Her life, in short, seemed as cozy as raingear on a winter beach. Reading Supergirl comics must have worked.

But there's kryptonite in everyone's world and a car accident left a flimsy rag doll behind it. Years of physical pain followed and, worse still, a total lack of humor. These days Diana has found her humor again and relies on it whenever her heart gets wrenched by how we treat the environment or each other. The hopeless romantic forges on.

She exhibits with the Group of Eight, attends the Banff Centre School of Fine Arts, and has illustrated Wildflowers of Canada, by Tim Fitzharris, published by Oxford University Press.

I have loved a lot of places that are now gone. I think it takes courage to keep on loving nature in the face of all the loss. It's hard to keep losing the things you love. And I really mean love.

I once heard melancholy defined as the feeling of loss when you don't know what has been lost. When you come to a place like Carmanah, you realize what has been missing. The richness is tremendous.

I've never been in a rainforest like this and I'm absolutely astounded. The trees are like old warriors. Each one is an individual; each one has character. They are so old it's hard to even comprehend their age. It's our history, Canada's history, and these monarchs are still alive.

It's important that places like this can exist and be preserved. It's exciting to know that we saw marbled murrelets and that they nest here safely. It's pure joy. I have felt like a babe in the woods walking around in God's country.

This valley should be preserved right from the top of the watershed. You can't just preserve a small portion. A friend of mine had her home washed away when the river they lived beside became a torrent of mud and stumps from the freshly logged hillsides above her. The trees had held the slopes intact for hundreds of years; without the vegetation, the rain scoured everything away. I wouldn't want this to happen to Carmanah

The piece I have done is about the conflict of emotions I felt when I was in Carmanah: the awe, the excitement, and the beauty mixed with the fear of loss. It is about having the courage to love with all your heart when the future is not known.

Diana Thompson

Woman in the Trees
mixed media
56 x 76 cm (22" x 30")

William Townsend

From the beginning of his career, William Townsend had the satisfaction of seeing his work sell quickly. His art continues to be collected by both Canadian and international corporations and he was recently featured along with twelve other artists in the hour-long CBC television special Painting Canada. *An impressive list of galleries carry his work across Canada and he is also represented in California.*

He knew from an early age that he would make his mark as a painter. His formal art education began after high school: from Vancouver to New York he absorbed as much as he could about design, subject, and composition.

After spending time overseas with the magazine industry, he returned to Canada, where he continued in the communications field until an art agent told him he could sell everything Townsend could paint. He has never regretted trading his briefcase for a brush and paints.

Townsend's paintings record the contrast in the sky, the angular beauty of the mountains, the ever-changing mood of the rivers, and the rugged surface of the woods. Each deliberate stroke is part of an evolving work of art that captures time in a very personal way. His paintings speak of more than just beauty; they speak of freedom—a freedom found only within ourselves.

I'm getting tired of living a life trying to figure out what I can eat and what I can't and where I can go for a walk and where I can't. I'm really used to freedom and I've been noticing it disappearing. I took friends, who were visiting from Germany, to Long Beach and they commented on the devastation at the side of the road. Then the CBC came from Montreal to do a film and the same thing happened; they were horrified. I started thinking, "This is the island I live on. How long is it going to be before I can't go and do any painting on my own island?"

There are beautiful places and there is no reason to knock them down. When I go to Europe, every once in a while an old building is missing, but it happens very seldom. They're trying to save Venice because it's beautiful. I don't see any reason why we can't save this forest. I'd like to bring my grandchild here—I don't have a grandchild yet—but I'd like to show him or her the Carmanah.

A lot of people don't realize when they are younger and very involved in their jobs that all of this exists. It's like the person who can't enjoy his time off until he retires, and by the time he retires, it's too late to enjoy himself. It's the same with a lot of people who never come here.

I've really felt that freedom I was talking about. I really found it. I've been able to wander off and walk through the woods. I feel like I've been rejuvenated. One of the most incredible things, too, has been meeting people from so many walks of life, all with different ideas and things they want to do.

I actually had a vision of what I was going to paint before I left; I pictured this huge butt of a tree in my mind. The very first day I got here, there was my tree; my tree was sitting there in the woods!

William Townsend

Big Tree, Carmanah Valley
oil on canvas
51 x 41 cm (20" x 16")

Roy Henry Vickers

Roy Henry Vickers is a West Coast native Indian artist whose name has become known worldwide for his unique graphic style. His clean lines, brilliant colors, and uncomplicated forms please the eye and allow the viewer to become involved in the interpretation of his work.

He was born in Greenville, British Columbia, in June 1946. His mother, of British ancestry, was a teacher and his father was a Tsimshian fisherman. The Vickers family lived in the ancient Tsimshian village of Kitkatla on the Northwest Coast of British Columbia, later moving to Hazelton and then to Victoria. Roy Vickers's interest, talent, and indeed destiny led him to the Gitanmaax School of Northwest Coast Indian Art at 'Ksan, near Hazelton. His studies there, coupled with hard work and determination, gradually developed a style that progressed from the traditional to his current unique and easily recognized designs.

A high point in his career came in 1987, when the government of British Columbia presented Her Majesty Queen Elizabeth II with an original painting, A Meeting of Chiefs, *at the Commonwealth heads of government meeting. Each of the government leaders received a limited edition silk-screen of the image.*

Vickers lives and works in Tofino, British Columbia, displaying his work in his Eagle Aerie Gallery, built in 1986 on the theme of a traditional West Coast Indian longhouse.

The Carmanah Valley, Clayoquot Sound, South Moresby Island, the Stein Valley: these are the few accessible virgin forests left in British Columbia today. When I see these pristine stands of timber, I cannot help but meditate on the first peoples of this great land and the respect they had for all living things, especially the forest and its wealth. The forest was then, and still is, a life-giving force. The trees hold the earth together when rain threatens to wash the soil into the spawning beds of the many species of salmon that frequent our rivers and streams. The branches provide shelter and homes for the birds and animals that live in our forests.

The Indians knew the importance of the forest and treated it with the reverence and respect it deserves. Homes, clothing, all manner of eating utensils, ropes, twine, hunting and fishing tools—all these things were obtained without killing the trees. A few planks were split from a tree, leaving it alive to provide for another generation. Bark was stripped from trees in small quantities so that life-giving sap could sustain the tree. This bark was fashioned into clothes, hats, and rope, even sleeping mats. Roots were dug, to be woven into hats and used for twine to bind fish hooks and hunting tools. Large ocean-going canoes were made from select mature trees. All of the products were made with minimal damage to the forest.

We must learn from the past before it is too late. We have treated the forest with disrespect far too long. We must realize the value of the few accessible virgin forests that remain. They are more valuable alive than dead. These few stands of timber are our heritage; they must be preserved for our children and the generations to come.

Roy H. Vickers

Carmanah
serigraph 1/50
66 x 51 cm (26" x 20")

1/50   CARMANAH

Morgan Warren

Born in Manchester, England, Morgan Warren immigrated with her family to Victoria, British Columbia, in 1957. Although she was a keen student of natural history from an early age, her formal studies focused mainly on literature and creative writing, first at the University of Victoria and later in London, England. She subsequently held a number of diverse jobs, including writer for a women's magazine.

In 1978 she finally combined her fascination for birds and animals with her lifelong hobby of watercolor painting and became a professional wildlife artist. This is a decision she has never regretted. Her paintings now hang in corporate and private collections from Toronto to San Francisco, and her limited edition fine art reproductions and art cards are distributed throughout North America. A hallmark of her work is her depiction of highly rendered subjects against misty, out-of-focus backgrounds that hint at the environment rather than portray it in detail.

Morgan Warren lives in Brentwood Bay, British Columbia, with her husband and three parrots, and works full time at her A-frame studio in Canoe Cove, thirty kilometres (nineteen miles) north of Victoria, at the tip of the scenic Saanich Peninsula.

At midnight I left my tent and walked along the river. Somewhere in the trees a flycatcher called repeatedly, its joy in the mood of spring undeterred by darkness. Above the forest's silhouette, the sky shone brightly with stars. I wondered if anyone out there was observing us, or whether we are too insignificant at this stage of our development to merit notice.

"Insignificant!" That is a thought to give us pause, in view of the arrogance some of us display in assuming that this planet's riches are here solely for our benefit. We are part of a vast symbiotic system, a living entity which is the entire globe —humans, animals, plants, microbes —all interacting and interdependent. To a degree this entity is self-maintaining and self-healing; it can withstand meteor impacts, massive solar disturbances, and more. But if attacked from within by man, it will be gravely harmed, even destroyed. The deforestation of our Earth is an attack on its living heart, and there are some who are fully aware of the price to be paid.

Those who say it is necessary to log the Carmanah Valley should take one clear night to walk the riverbank, breathe the cool, tree-scented air, and watch the stars. No matter how many times life might occur around those distant points of light, there will only ever be one Earth. If we do not learn to understand, respect, and cherish it for its own sake, we will never grow up and go forth from it.

Rainsong of the Varied Thrush

Where shadows kiss riverstones,
Darken the sparkle
Of dew-drops on moss,
I sing for the trees:

In the green dusk I whistle
Harmonies in half-tones,
A cadence of ages
For giants of time;

By quaver I measure
Their root-growth and sap-flow,
Fill hillside and valley
With my song's liquid echo

Which fades away slowly
Like a mist in the sun.

M. Morgan Warren

Rainsong of the Varied Thrush
watercolor
38 x 51 cm (15" x 20")

M. Morgan Warren

Alison Watt

Alison Watt grew up in Victoria, British Columbia, and spent several years in Vancouver, where she completed a degree in biology and worked as education coordinator at VanDusen Botanical Garden. These experiences, together with her work as a naturalist in parks across British Columbia and in Amazonian Peru, have shaped a deep appreciation of the natural world, which finds expression in her botanical paintings.

Watt has shown in recent years on Vancouver Island and in Vancouver with a group of seven other West Coast landscape and wildlife artists. Currently she lives in Nanaimo, where she works at home caring for her two small children—and painting when she can.

What is it about old-growth forest? Is it the quality of the light filtered through the high tree tops? The way bird song is absorbed by the heavily mossed forest floor? The change of scale when standing among monolithic trees?

In the Carmanah Valley, with clearcut and dusty road behind me, I was in an age-old forest.

Like most of the days that I have spent in old-growth rainforest, both temperate and tropical, the days I spent in Carmanah were some of my most memorable. I like to paint the detail of the forest floor. The little plants are sometimes forgotten when we talk about big trees. I remember hearing a company forester talking about how old-growth forests just rot and die, so that there's no useful wood anymore. Yet other organisms, though perhaps not economically valuable, are important parts of the ecosystem.

As I sat sketching the vegetation at the foot of a large spruce, the roar of logging equipment nearby was disturbing. Tracing tender stems and sun-spotted leaves, I knew that they could soon be crushed without a glance and that this square metre of life would be replaced with dry, blackened crust. The sound of chainsaws reminded me that what was happening in this small corner of Vancouver Island is part of an accelerating removal of the last primal forest all over the globe. The peaceful process of sketching the life of the Carmanah Valley was accompanied by a disquieting sense of urgency.

Wilderness all over the world is disappearing within our lifetimes. If we don't take care of our own old-growth forests, we can't really expect other countries of the world to protect their original forests. We need a synthesized, comprehensive plan that provides for a sustainable forest industry, so that every old-growth forest issue does not become a public debate.

Alison Watt

Forest Floor
watercolor on paper
52 x 44 cm (20½" x 17¼")

156

Jim Willer

Born in England, Jim Willer immigrated to Canada in 1947 and attended the Winnipeg School of Art. "Joe Plaskett taught there—the first committed artist I had ever met. He was articulate, and I intuited that I too must be, in the deepest sense, well-informed. Kenneth Clark expressed what I mean much more cogently: '. . . the greatest art has always been about something, a means of communicating some truth which is assumed to be more important than the art itself.' Whatever the fashions and fads in art, I've always believed that."

In 1953, Lawren Harris saw Willer's paintings in the Vancouver Art Gallery and offered to support his application for an overseas award. This was a critical juncture in Jim's life. He found the Royal Academy of Art in Amsterdam stifling, but he learned how and what to paint by wandering Europe. In 1955 he joined Joe Plaskett and Tak Tanabe on a painting tour from Paris to Greece.

Willer's work is found in public and private collections across Canada, including the Winnipeg, Vancouver, and Victoria art galleries. He won a Canada Council fellowship for sculpture in 1966 and a competition to create a sculpture for the BCIT campus in Burnaby, British Columbia. His novel Paramind *(McClelland & Stewart, 1973) shared first prize for literature in the* Canada 2000 A.D. *competition.*

Some Carmanah spruce began life in the Middle Ages when God still steered the ship—long before Renaissance Man seized the helm. We're still not back on course and the war on the environment grows exponentially. Our attempt to prevent the destruction of the Carmanah forest is merely a skirmish in the global war between the friends and foes of nature. It's an archaic war—the bread and circuses of Rome cost North Africa its forests, and later, Venice diminished the forests of Europe.

But let us not be too hard on *Homo sapiens*—we didn't invent ourselves, nor our devilish ingenuity, nor our world! So why assume that a planet with a continuous history of remarkable actors (the whale, shrew, orangutan, and the rest of the cast) might fail, simply because a few leading, hairless actors stood up on two legs and rewrote the script?

If we're sapient enough we'll go to the forests—a paradigm of superior technology:

- Complete recycling of old and broken machines—not a twig or leaf is wasted.
- No fouling of the workspace to slow the millennial production of future spruce.
- The powerhouse does not pollute nor harm, being a safe 90 million miles away.
- The technology has endured 2 billion years.

Pessimism, with its nineteenth-century mechanistic philosophy, pervades the West with its recipe for the origin of life as a proto-amino soup and a flash of lightning. I prefer my own philosophy: all that is necessary to produce life-forms and mind is inherent in matter itself. Because it is programmed to do so (on planets where conditions are favorable), matter evolves into life-forms which ultimately think for themselves and reflect upon their place in the universe.

This hypothesis inspires us by the realization that we are participants in a remarkably creative act, rather than the outcome of a chance arrangement of atoms, and is compatible with the laws of physics and evolution. It should also inspire us to assert another phase of our programming: that of stewardship over the rest of the global ecosystem as its guardian, not its enemy.

Jim Willer

Carmanah Series No. 1,
Gaia's Not for Burning
pastel on paper
65 x 92 cm (25½" x 36¼")

GAIA'S NOT FOR BURNING

Marla Wilson

Born in Wales in 1945, Marla Wilson came to Alberta in 1946. Showing an early aptitude for art, she began art classes at the age of six and became a professional artist at the age of eighteen. She attended classes at the Edmonton Art Gallery, Shepy National School of Art, University of Alberta extension, and studied sculpture at the Northern Alberta Institute of Technology. Within a few years of attaining professional standing, her work was being seen around the world—in New Zealand, Great Britain, Ghana, Bahrein, Chile, Peru, and Japan—as well as being sought for many corporate collections.

Wilson works in acrylics, primarily painting highly detailed images of North American wildlife. Her style has been influenced by Lansdowne, Bateman, and Wyeth. She is known particularly for the feeling and mood that can be discovered in her pieces. Her work is now available in limited edition fine art reproductions which quickly sell out across North America.

Wildlife conservation programs are very important to her and she is currently involved with and donating her work to Ducks Unlimited and other organizations oriented to preserving the environment. Nature and art are Marla's life, and hiking the Carmanah Valley, alpine areas, and coastal areas are exciting pastimes for this Vancouver Island resident.

A trip to the Carmanah Valley is a visit to a forest wonderland of breathing beauty. Imagination runs wild, jumping from the fantasy of having a Swiss Family Robinson way of life there to the automatic appreciation of an artist's eye for the flowing abstract shapes and rugged textures of the moss and the tree structures.

This area has taken thousands of years to evolve. I thought about what a thrill and great privilege it was to be there, and then suddenly it occurred to me that it shouldn't be a privilege. It should be a right. The tallest trees in Canada should remain, and everyone should have the right to see them. Besides the tall Sitka spruce, cedar, fir, and hemlock, there are cedar trees estimated to be over a thousand years old.

I want to create in my painting, *Carmanah Harmony*, the feeling of the old and new, with the old-growth Sitka spruce and the new-born Columbian black-tailed deer. I also want to portray the Carmanah Valley, a historic treasure, as very much alive.

Trees have always had a special part in my wildlife paintings. They are often a focal point before the animal or bird. So the rainforest of the Carmanah was an exceptional sight to see. A trip back there this year will be a must, and I only hope there is a magnificent valley left for our relatives to see in the future.

Marla Wilson

Carmanah Harmony
acrylic on board
61 x 46 cm (24" x 18")

Jack Wise

Jack Wise studied at the New Orleans School of Fine Arts, graduated from Washington University in St. Louis, and completed graduate work at Florida State University in 1955. During this time he absorbed the prevailing abstract expressionist style of painting.

In 1963, conscious of a need to restructure his approach to art, he immigrated to Canada and farmed in British Columbia. Like many contemporary artists, Wise was attracted to Asian art traditions and in 1966 studied with Tibetan painting masters in India.

His paintings are firmly anchored in his experiences of nature. He probes the deeper levels of the human psyche—levels hidden to the more usual kind of abstract paintings. This explains the appeal of his work to those who have retained the wonderful ability of children to respond purely on instinctual levels. The mystery of transcendence, the joyful tonality, and the deep harmony that emerge from his works suggest a world of transforming peace.

Wise has exhibited widely in the United States, Canada, Mexico, and Europe, and his works are represented in numerous collections. He has taught at the Layton School of Art, San Miguel Allende in Mexico, the Victoria College of Art and the University of Calgary. In recent years he has moved throughout British Columbia and now lives on Denman Island.

A growing number of people in the world realize that nature is our mirror of health as a species. It must not be broken by bottom-line short-term profit, lest we lose our viability as favored children of great natural forces that we are just beginning to comprehend.

The Carmanah Valley is only a small watershed in one of the largest countries in the world, yet it contains thousands of years of natural development untouched by human exploitation. As guardians of Earth's vitality, the native peoples have watched over it well. Now newcomers who have a long history of conspicuous consumption are planning to destroy it. Large corporate forces dedicated to clear-cut profit have effectively propagandized their employees into the belief that it is the "preservationists" who threaten their livelihood, and not profit-maximizing automation. Seeing one giant log-loader at work displacing a crew of workers convinces one beyond doubt that giant machines can only clear-cut; it takes careful, skilled humans to selectively log. Without effective opposition from enlightened citizenry, the men behind large-profit empires will leave the Carmanah a wasteland.

A fine clean creek runs through the valley floor. Birds here sing as though inspired. Dotting the valley are groves of Sitka spruce ascending to world-record heights. This unique ecosystem contains a pristine beauty beyond price, and it is fast disappearing here in Canada and around the world, along with biological information crucial to the rejuvenation of our blighted Earth.

The Carmanah Valley and its watershed must be preserved through law as a non-negotiable resource owned jointly by all Canadians. It must be a legacy to our descendants and a model of our awareness that the health of the Earth is fundamental to our survival on it.

Jack Wise

Grove
gouache on paper
26 x 36 cm (10" x 14")

Robbin Yager

Robbin Yager was born in Ontario but grew up in Alberta, where her entertainment was walking train rails to nowhere and roaming the woods playing cowboy. The contact with wild things influenced a dreamy childhood and developed in her a great respect for the workings of nature.

Art school taught her to emulate minimalism and adore abstract expressionism but light and color became the greatest influences on her etchings and drawings. After graduating she drifted through several jobs and then escaped to India and Nepal, where cynicism was replaced by a faith in the endurance of the world. Upon returning, she worked at various museums and galleries across Canada. In Toronto, Geraldine Davis represents Yager's prints and drawings and works hard for her cause.

Yager lived in Vancouver for three years, but the longing for a secure studio and the Rocky Mountains brought her back to Calgary. Her work reflects a respect for the perfection of nature (the nature of perfection) and the right of the natural world to determine its own existence.

Wild places are always special for me. In fact, I spend a good deal of my time thinking of them and planning my escape from people.

Why then, when placed on the small gravel bar at Camp Heaven with some forty artists and another twenty support staff, was I not ready to run in alarm to a more remote situation? The fact is, I felt no strain at all. Carmanah seemed to welcome us as its allies and the images the valley gave us became our weapons of hope.

When I consider my feelings about the experience in the Carmanah Valley, they are of privilege, appreciation, and longing. I took the feelings conveyed to me by my companions and gave them and my own thoughts back to the forest, the river, and the gravel bars. I was falling in love. Even the rocks bewitched me. My infatuation remains, and to this day I have an overwhelming sense that the valley has breathed strong medicine into my heart.

I would mourn the death of this remarkable valley as I would a dear friend. If it is not allowed to live out its long life according to its own innate rhythm, I won't despair, as one loss fuels the need for more victories. In the end I know that what is right will triumph.

Robbin Yager

Birds Fly Up, Fish Draw Near
etching
90 x 35 cm (35½" x 13¾")

If a Tree Falls...
Bruce Cockburn

rain forest
mist and mystery
teeming green
green brain facing lobotomy
climate control centre for the world
ancient cord of coexistence
hacked by parasitic greedhead scam—
from Sarawak to Amazonas
Costa Rica to mangy B.C. hills—
cortege rhythm of falling timber.

What kind of currency grows in these new deserts,
these brand new flood plains?

If a tree falls in the forest does anybody hear?
If a tree falls in the forest does anybody hear?
Anybody hear the forest fall?

Cut and move on
Cut and move on
take out trees
take out wildlife at a rate of a species every single day
take out people who've lived with this for 100,000 years—
inject a billion burgers worth of beef—
grain eaters—methane dispensers—

through thinning ozone,
waves fall on wrinkled earth—
gravity, light, ancient refuse of stars,
speak of a drowning—
but this, this is something other.
busy monster eats dark holes in the spirit world
where wild things have to go
to disappear
forever

Bruce Cockburn

*Canadian singer-songwriter Bruce Cockburn focuses on
political and environmental issues and is known world-wide
for his powerful lyrics.*

If A Tree Falls © 1988 Golden Mountain Music Corp.
Words and music by Bruce Cockburn.
Taken from the True North album Big Circumstance.
Reproduced with permission.

Canadian Cataloging in Publication Data

Carmanah: artistic visions of an ancient rainforest

1. Carmanah Valley (B.C.) – Description and travel – Views.
2. Natural history – British Columbia – Carmanah Valley.
I. Western Canada Wilderness Committee.

FC3845.C37C37 1989   917.11'34   C89-091473-3
F1089.C37C37 1989

ISBN 0-9692230-5-6

Production Credits

Executive producer: Ken Budd
Project coordinator: Arne Hansen
Designer: Alex Green
Interviewer/writer/text coordinator: Sherry Kirkvold
Editor: Elaine Jones
Expedition coordinator: Mark Hobson
Art photographer: Trevor Mills
Expedition photographers: Trevor Mills
                           Kevin Oke
                           Jay Squelch
                           Kaj Svensson
Other photographers not previously mentioned:
                           Jeff Gibbs
                           Gloria Graham
Art coordinators: Annette Garm
                   Fiona Gold
Electronic imaging and color separators:
   Zenith Graphics Limited
Printer: Hemlock Printers Ltd.
Binder: North-West Book Co. Ltd.

Photo Credits

Page 2: Adrian Dorst. Page 4: Ian Mackenzie. Page 6: (clockwise from upper left corner; centre photo last) 1, 2, 4, 7: Joe Foy; 3: Kevin Oke; 5: Ian Mackenzie; 6: Leo Degroot; 8: Ken Lay. Page 8: Gary Fiegehen. Page 24: (clockwise from upper left) *Artists at work* – 1: Jack Wise; 2: Erika Kertesz-Green; 3: Diana Thompson; 4: Drew Burnham; 5: Toni Onley; 6: Robert Bateman; 7: Arnold Shives; 8: Ross Bollerup. *Photographers* – 1,4,6: Kaj Svensson; 2, 3, 5, 7, 8: Jay Squelch. Page 167: Mark Hobson.

The Paper Stock

This book is printed on a Swedish dioxin-free paper. No such coated paper is currently available in North America. After an exhaustive search, the Wilderness Committee decided to buy an oxygen-bleached paper from Håfreströms AB.

Dioxins, highly toxic pollutants, are produced in technologically outdated pulp and paper mills when chlorine combines with organic substances. These dioxins become concentrated as they proceed through the food chain. In British Columbia, large parts of our valuable coastal fishery have been closed by the federal government because of dioxin and other pulp mill pollutants. We felt that it was important to print this book on an environmentally sound paper stock. The best news was that, even with extra shipping costs, the Swedish product was competitively priced with contaminated domestic paper.

Publisher:

Western Canada Wilderness Committee
20 Water Street,
Vancouver, B.C. V6B 1A4
(604) 683-8220

Producer:

SummerWild Productions
2202 1275 Pacific Street, Vancouver, B.C. V6E 1T6
(604) 681-0015

Distributor:
Raincoast ⏏ Books
Raincoast Books
112 East 3rd Avenue, Vancouver, B.C. V5T 1C8
(604) 873-6581

Printed in Canada